ISBN-13: 978-1548629137

ISBN-10: 1548629138

Printed by CreateSpace, An Amazon.com Company

www.createsuite.com

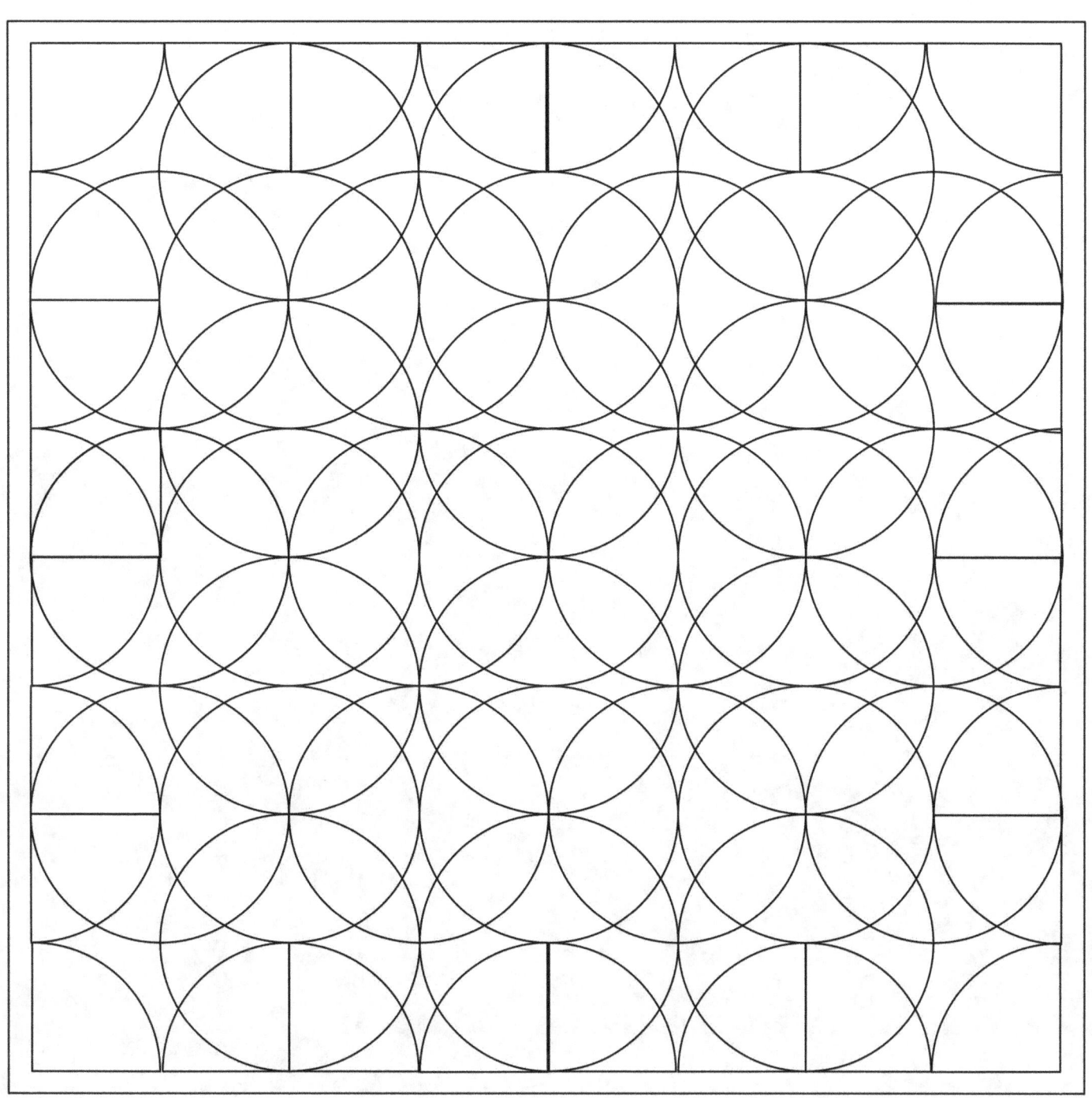

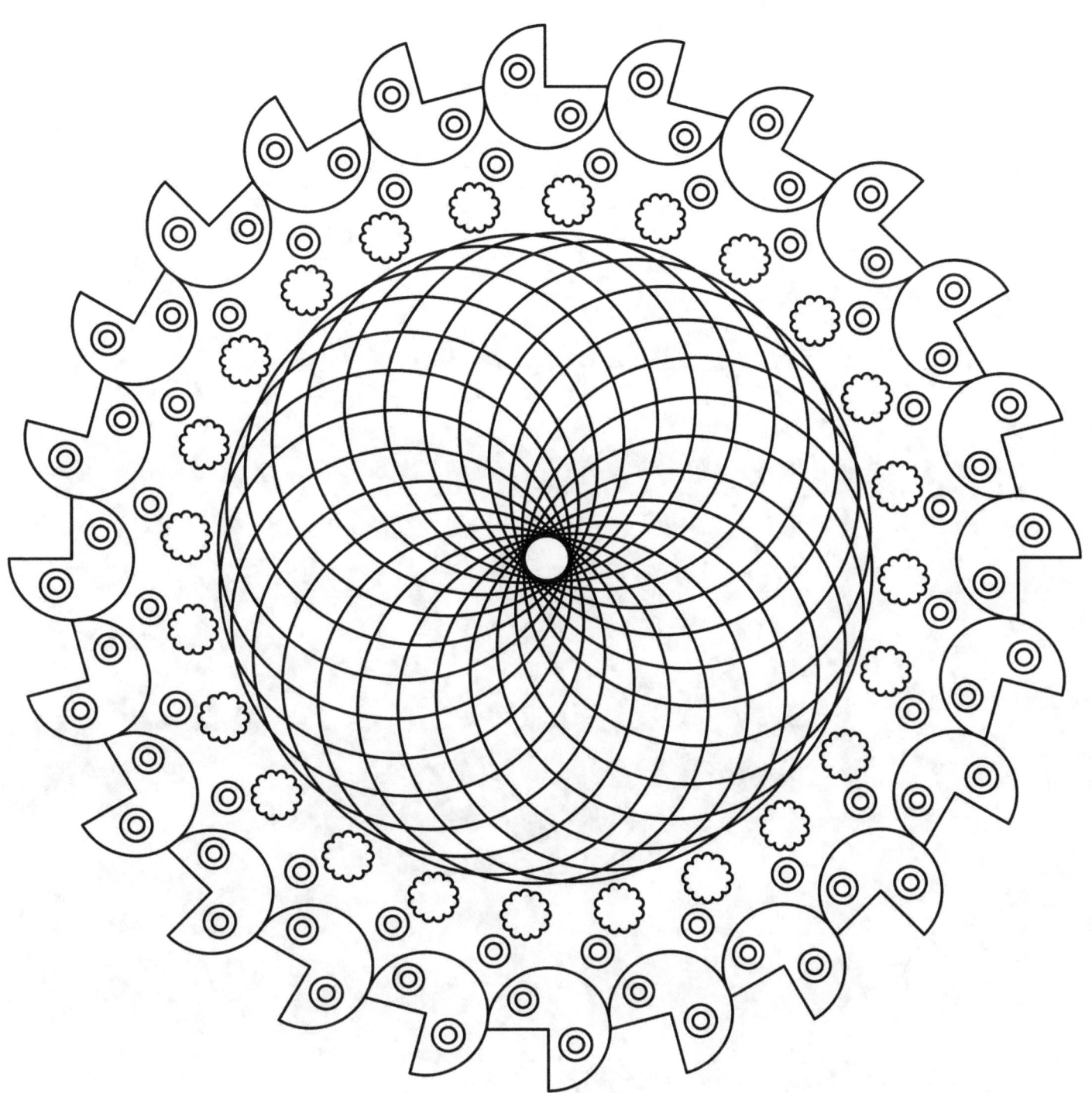

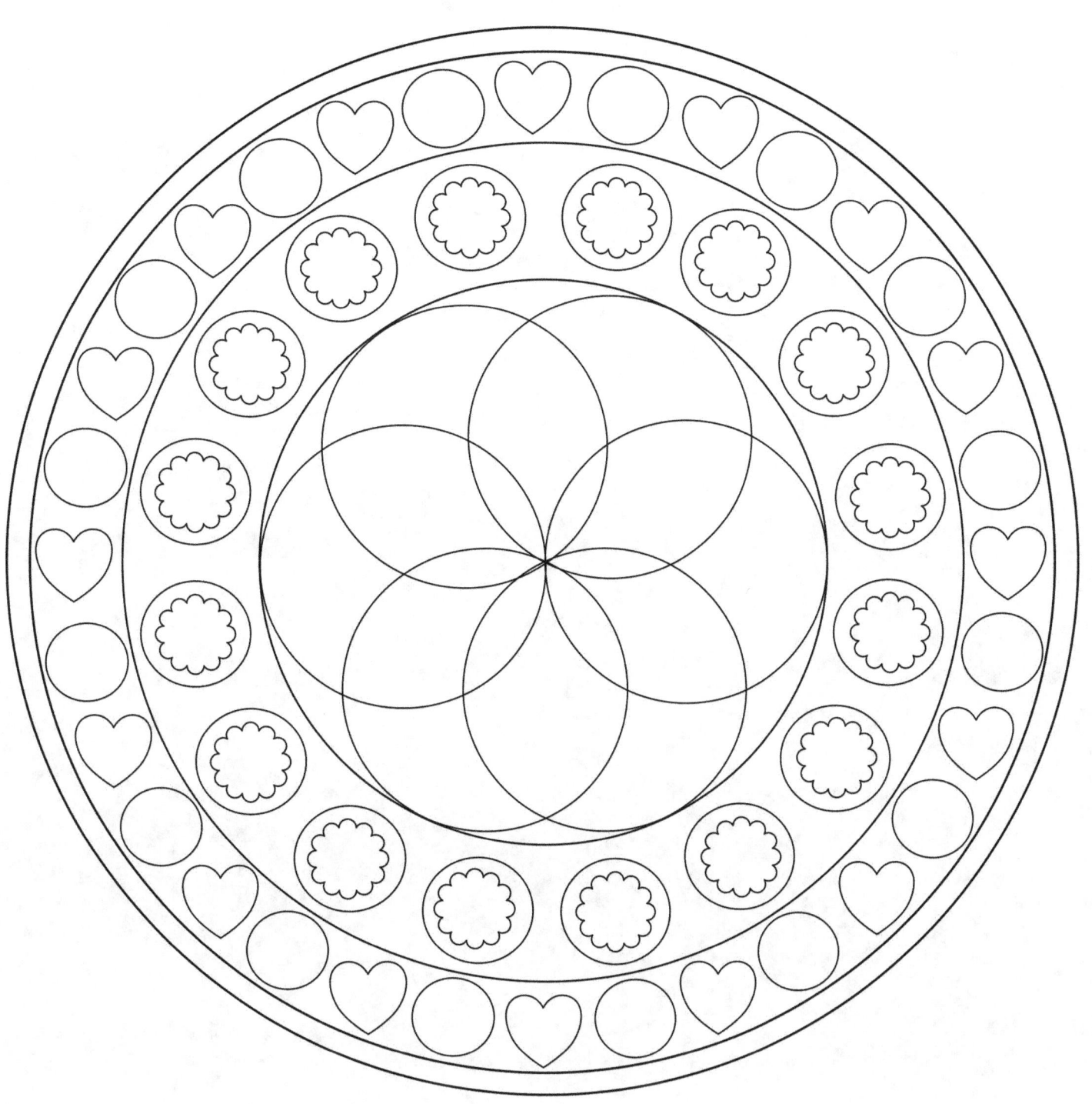

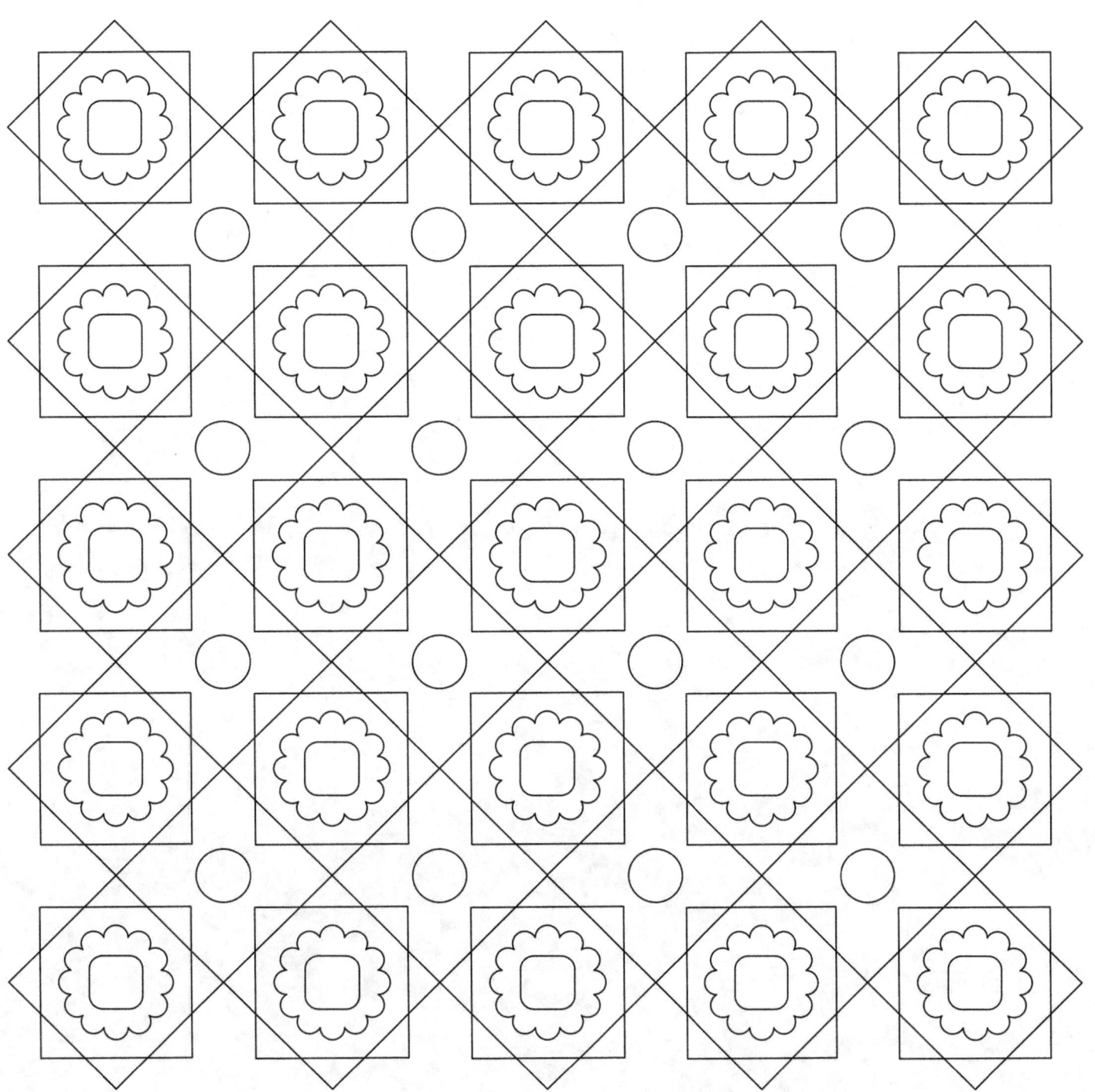

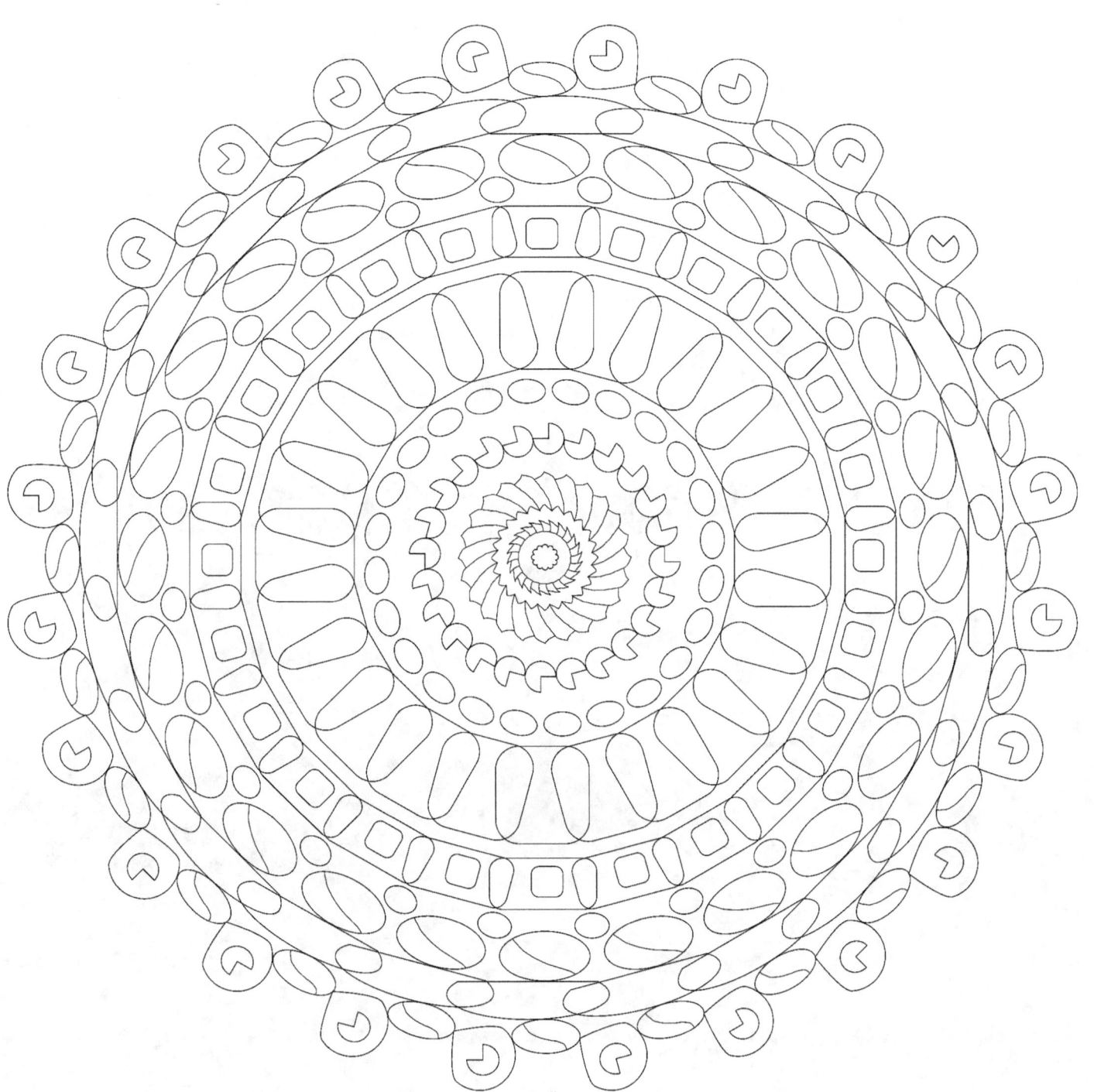

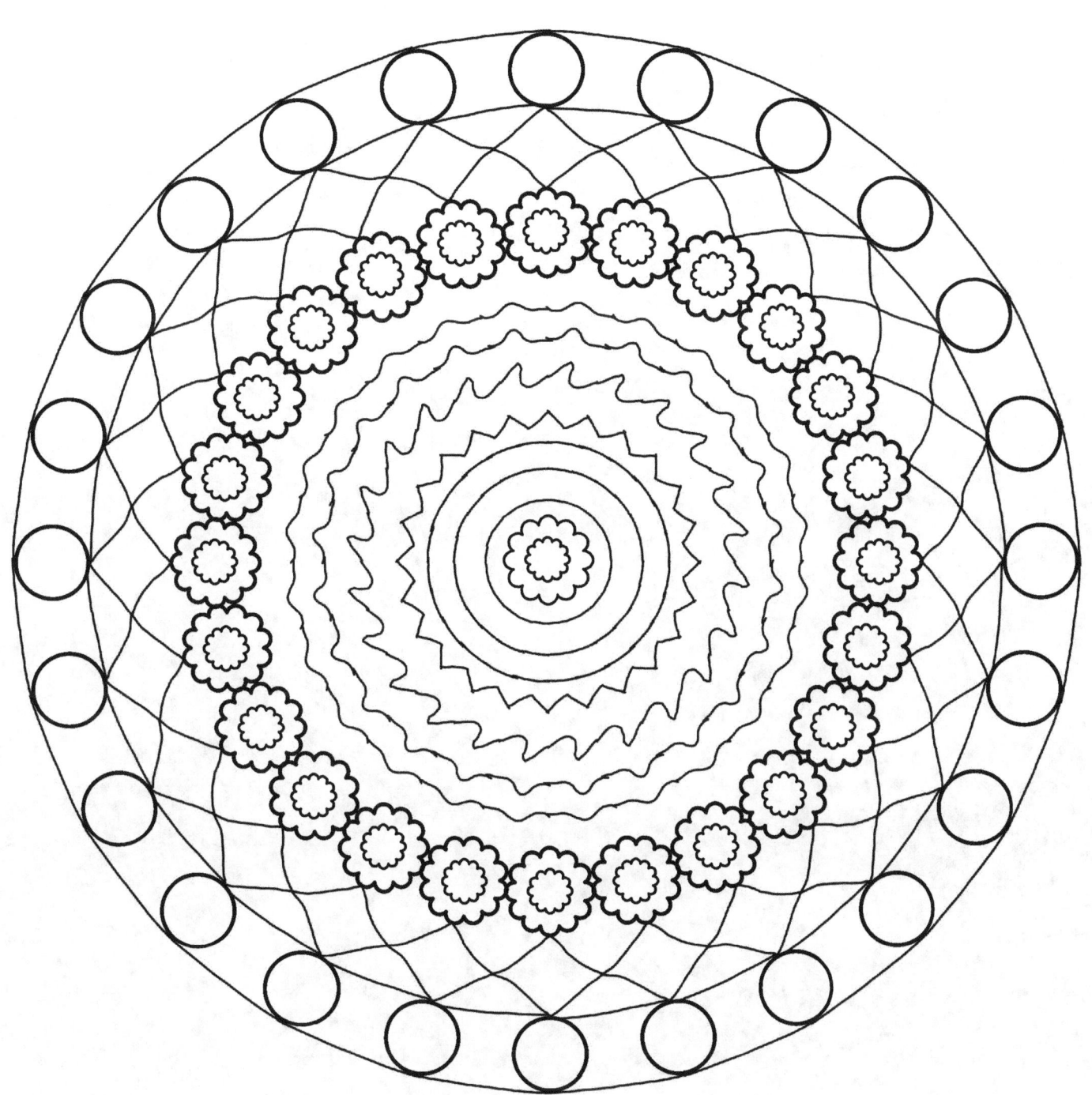

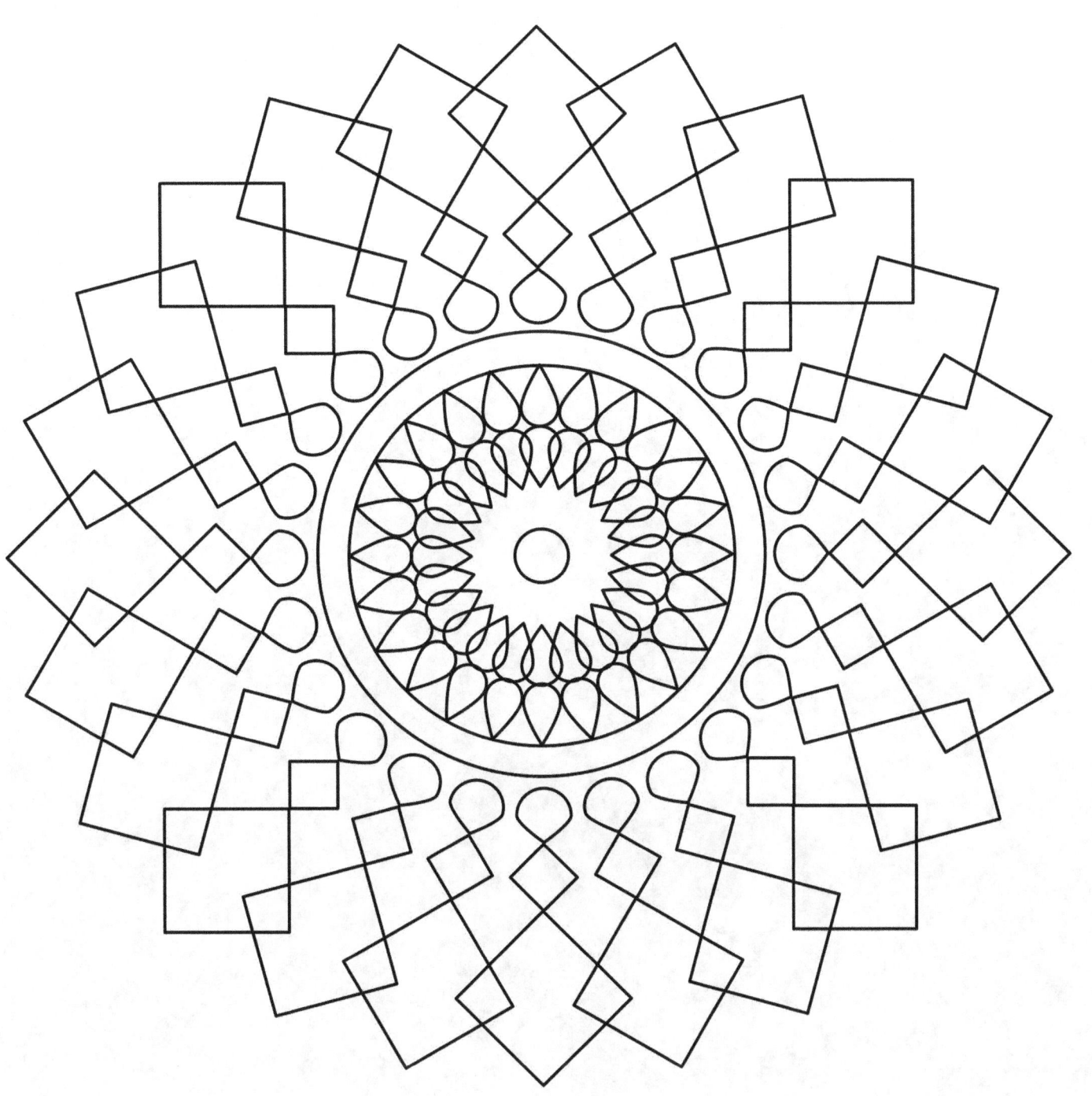

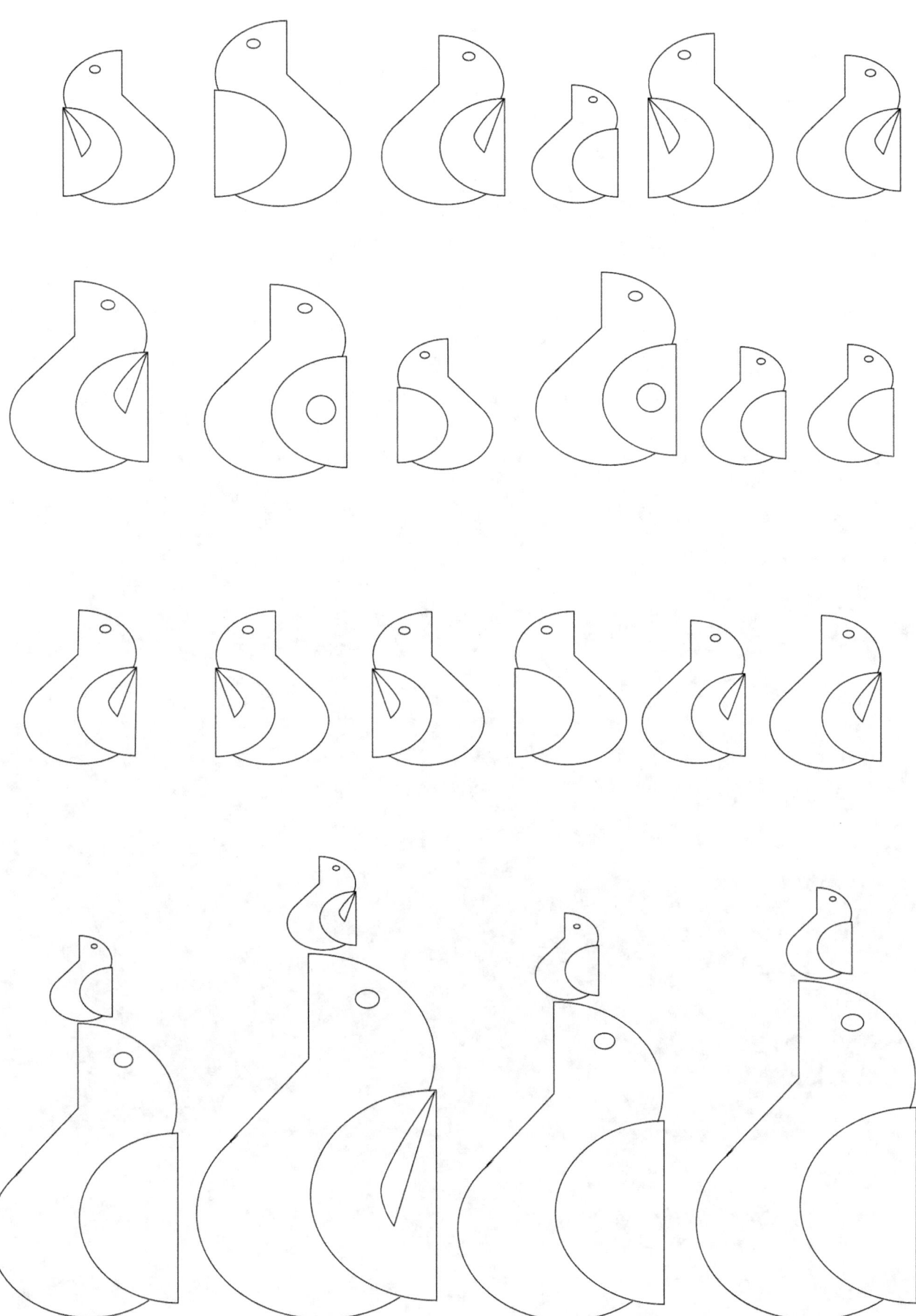

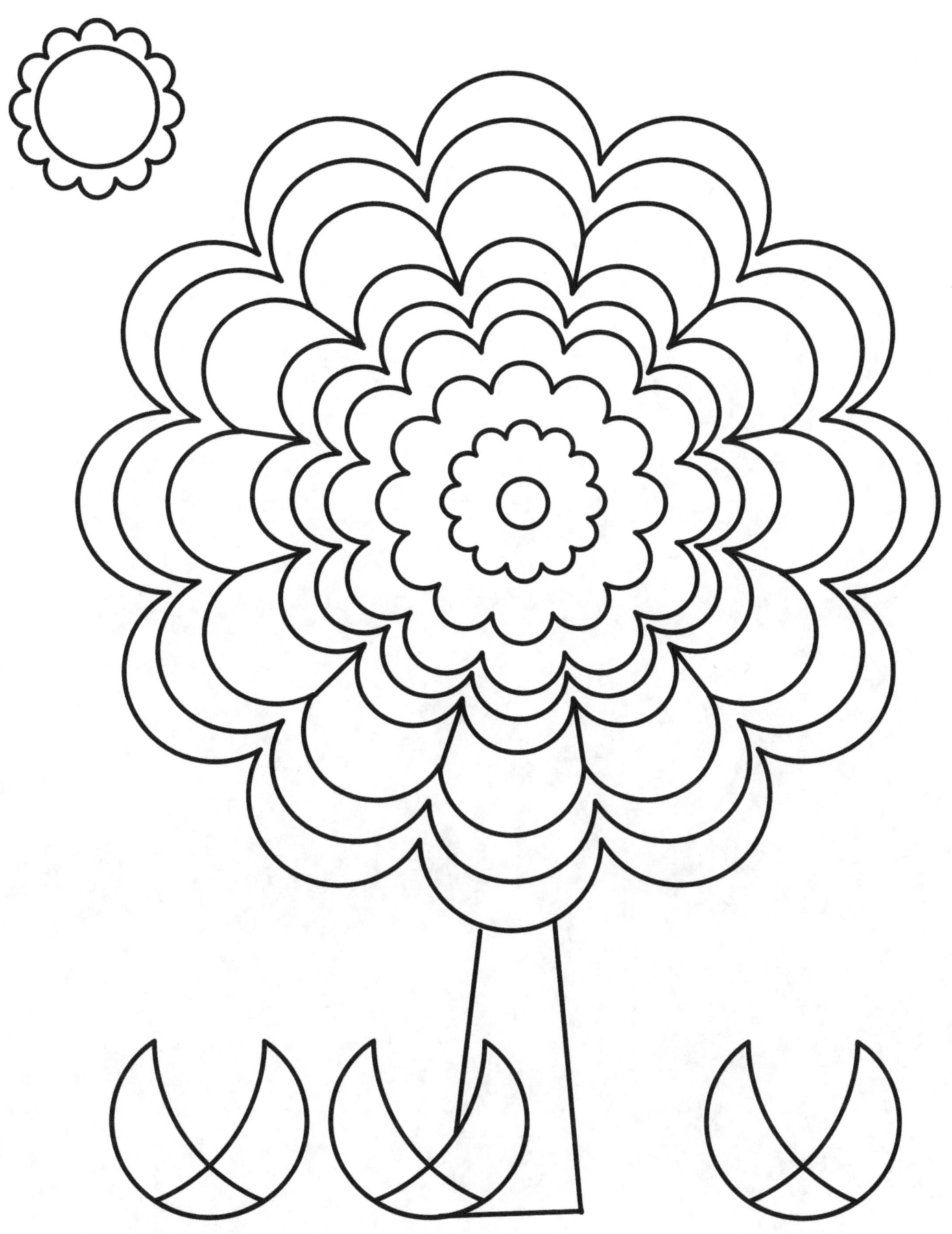

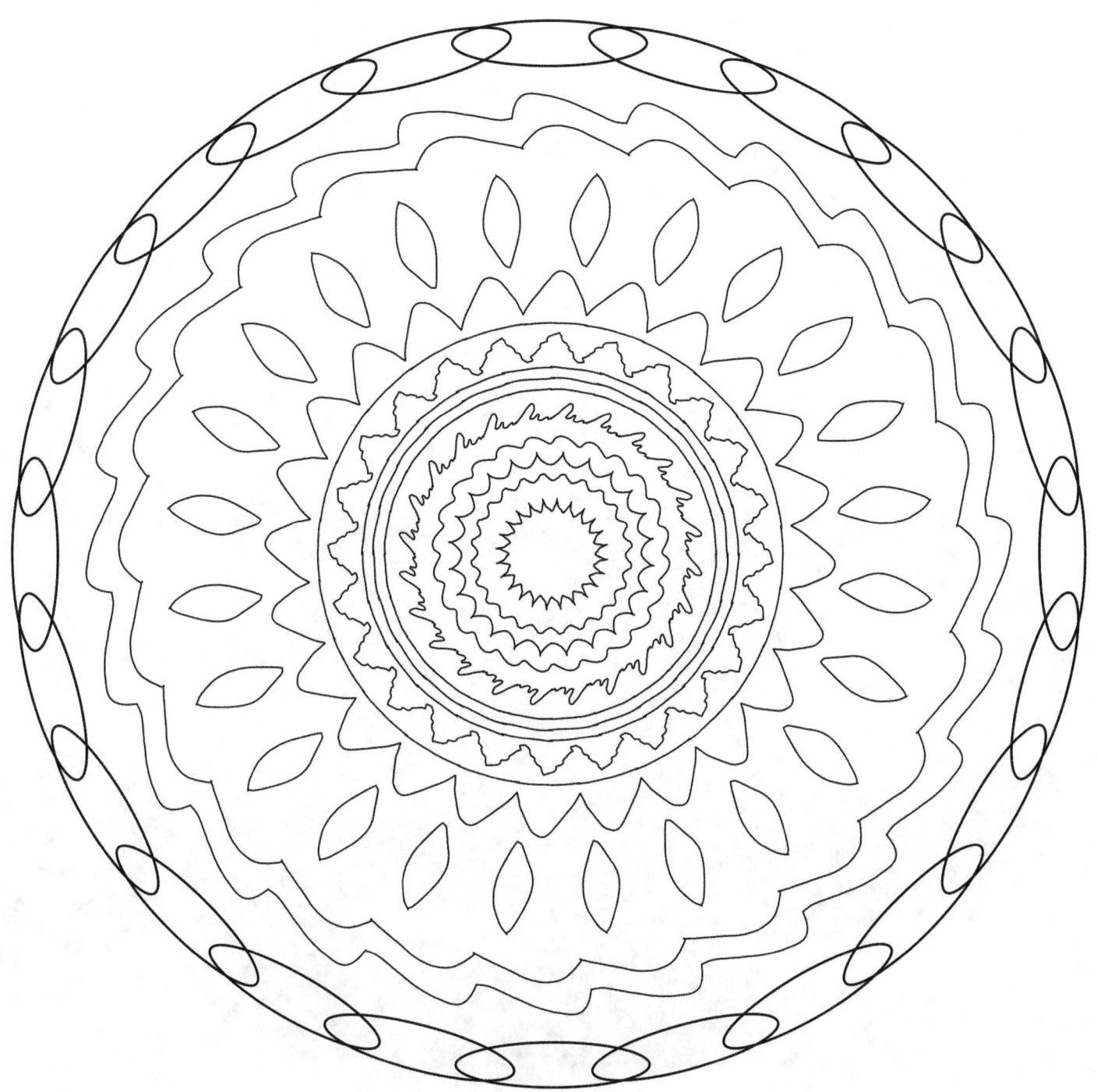

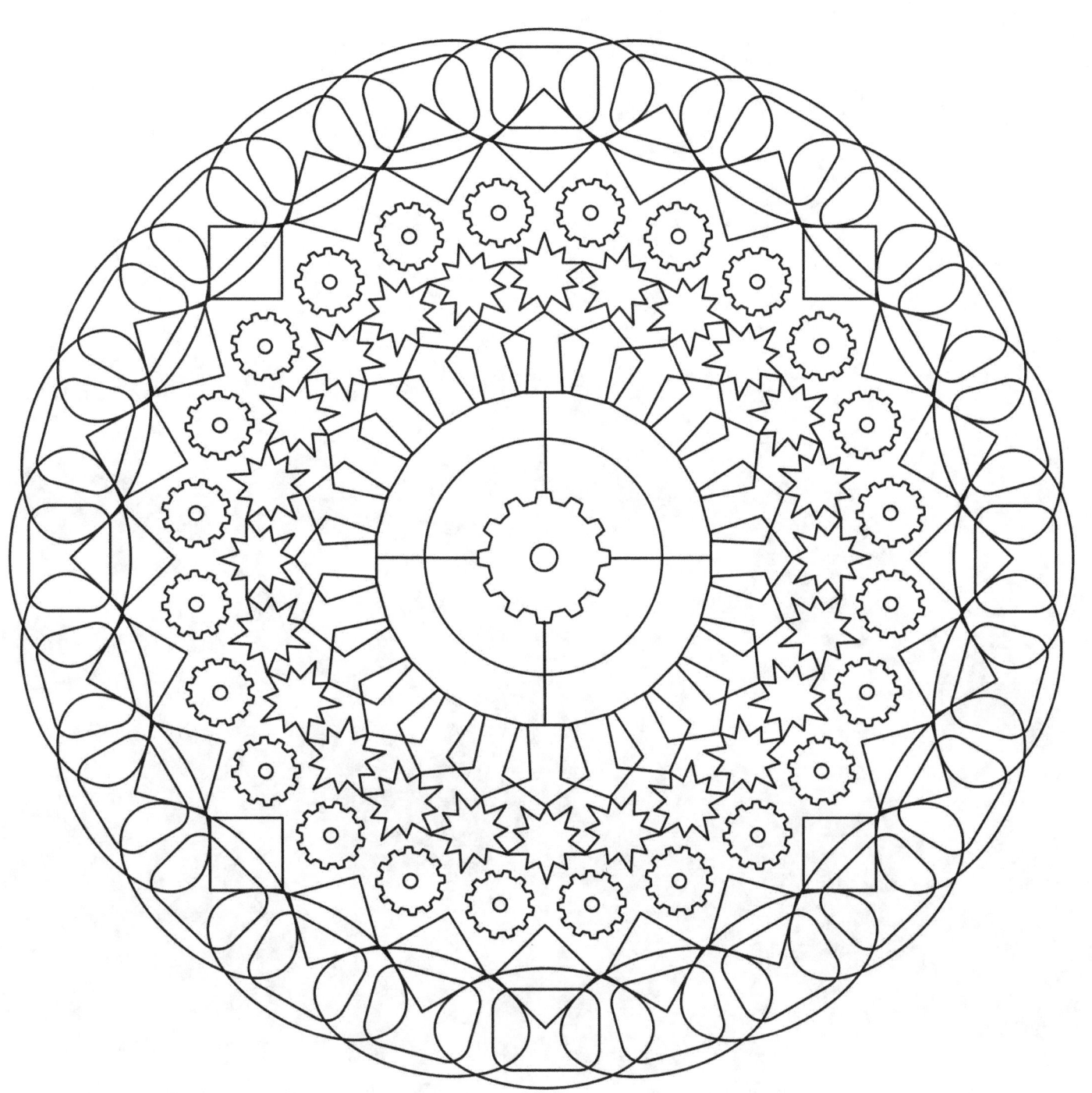

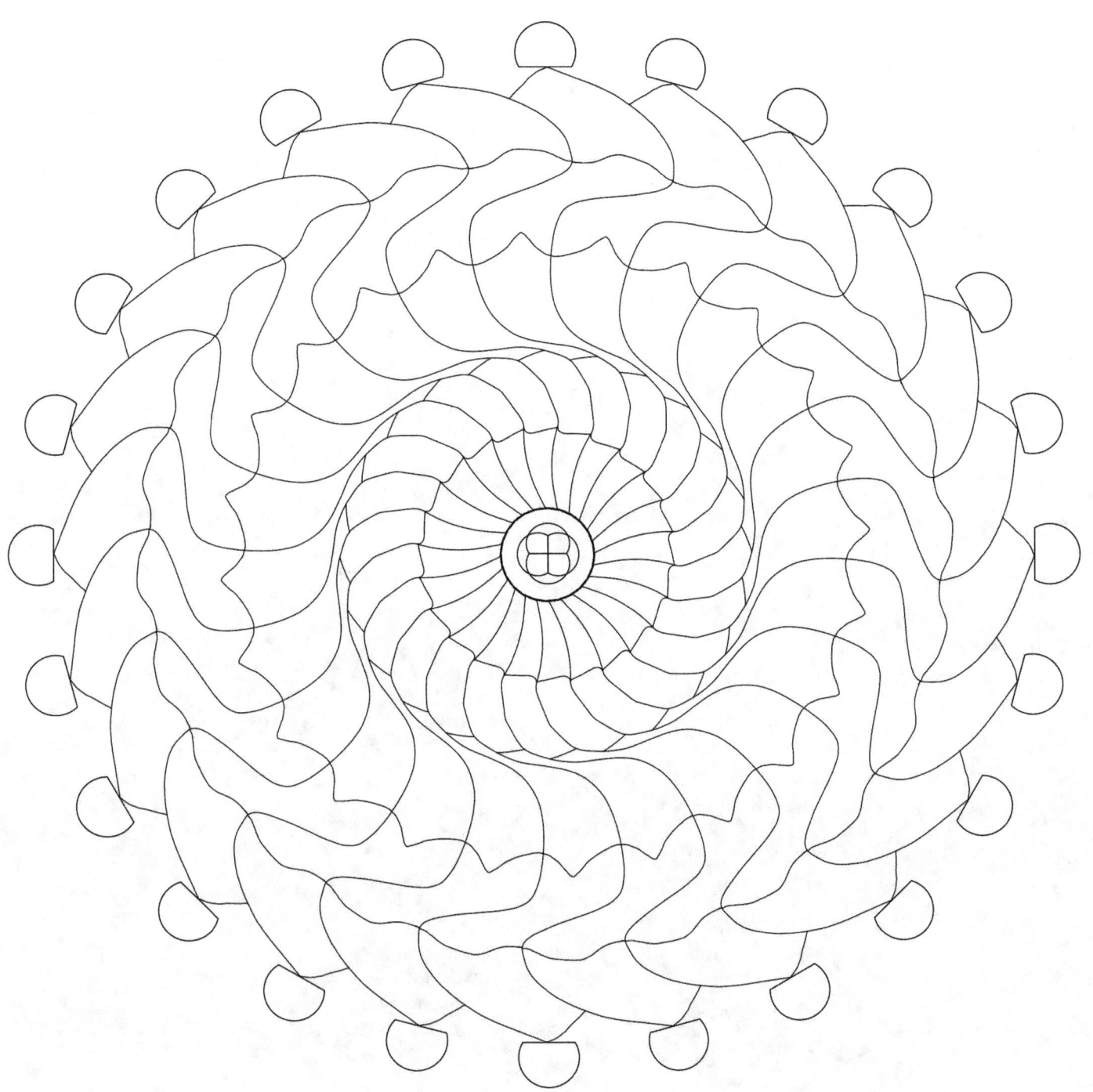

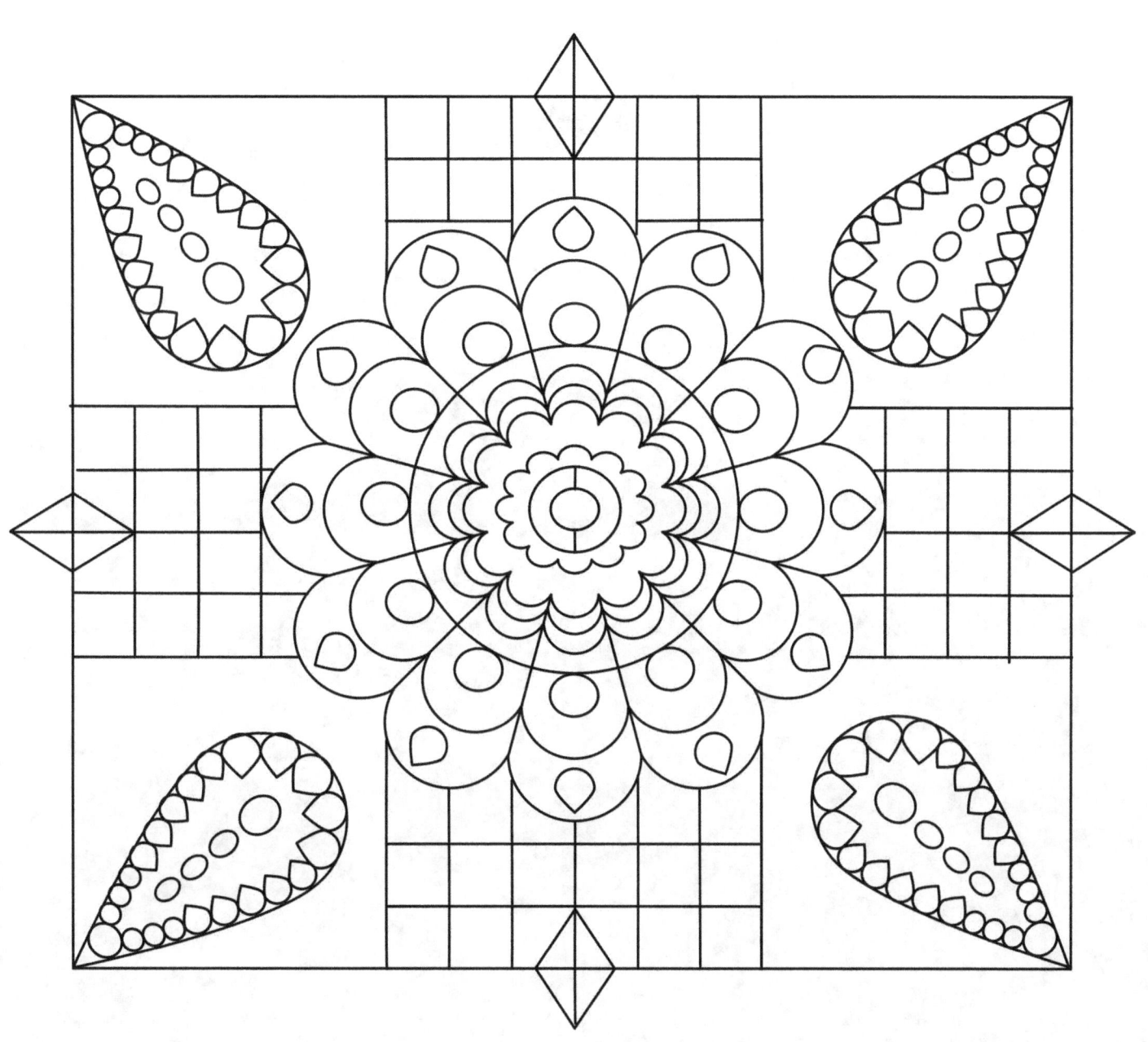

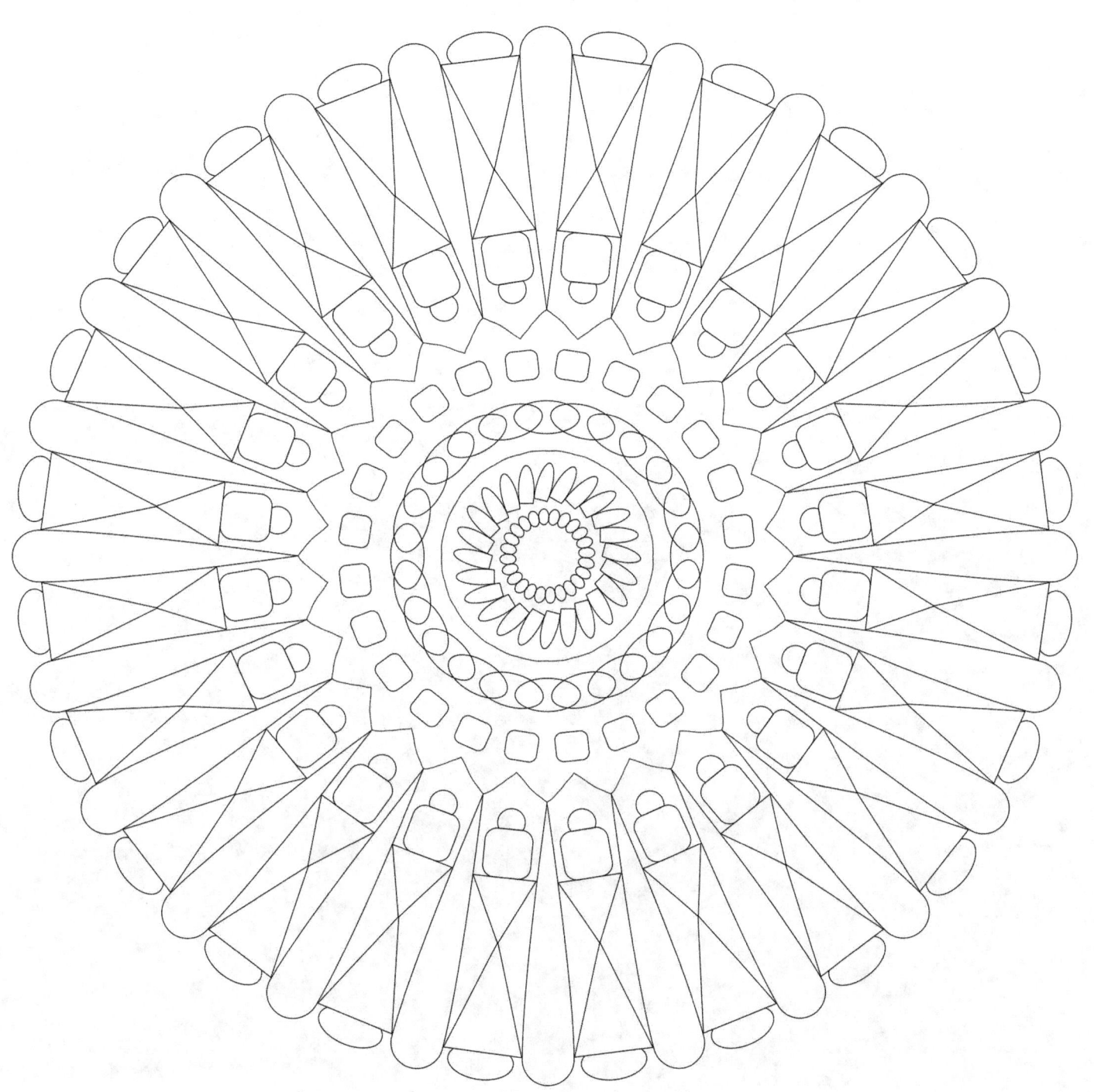

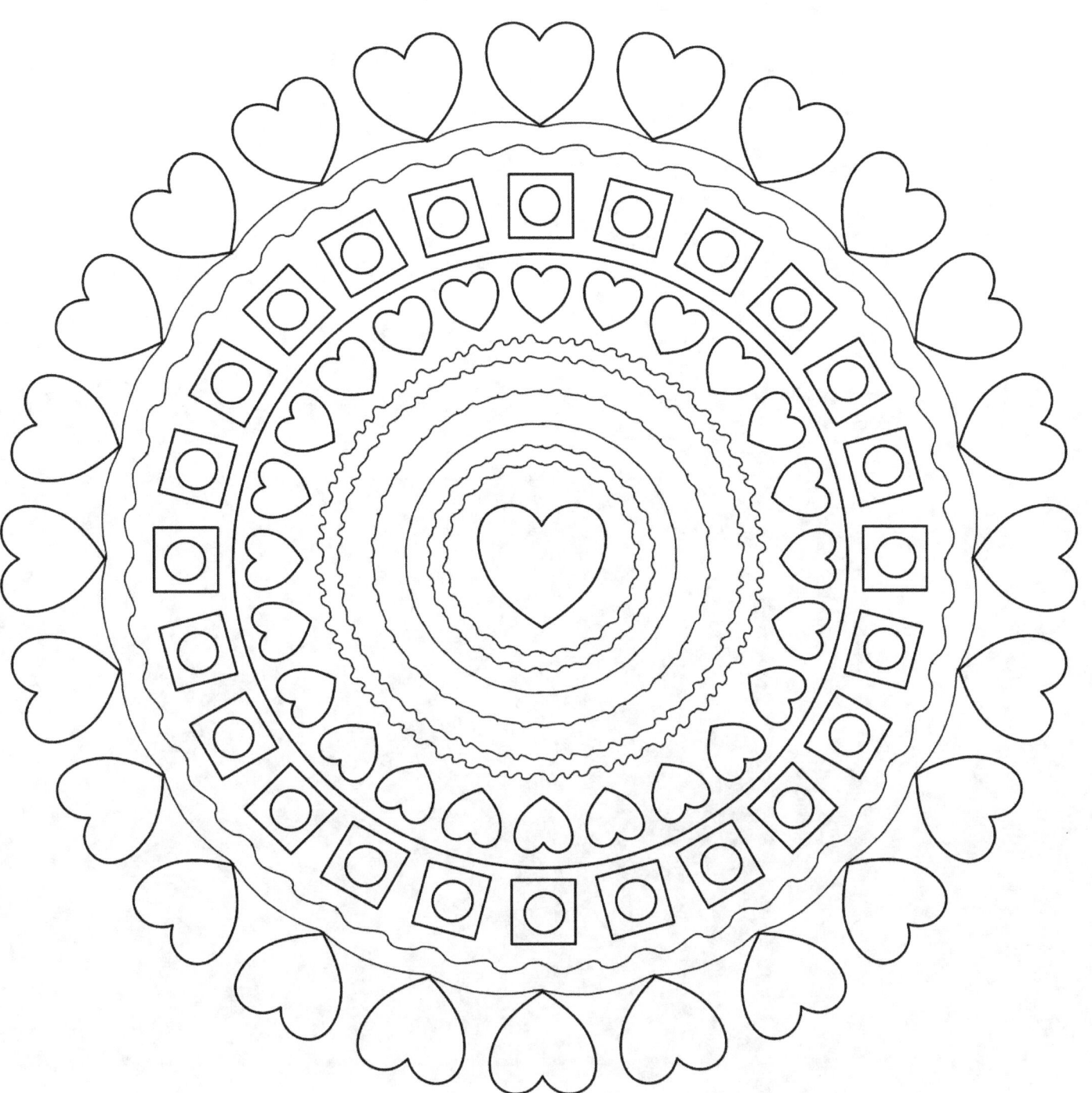

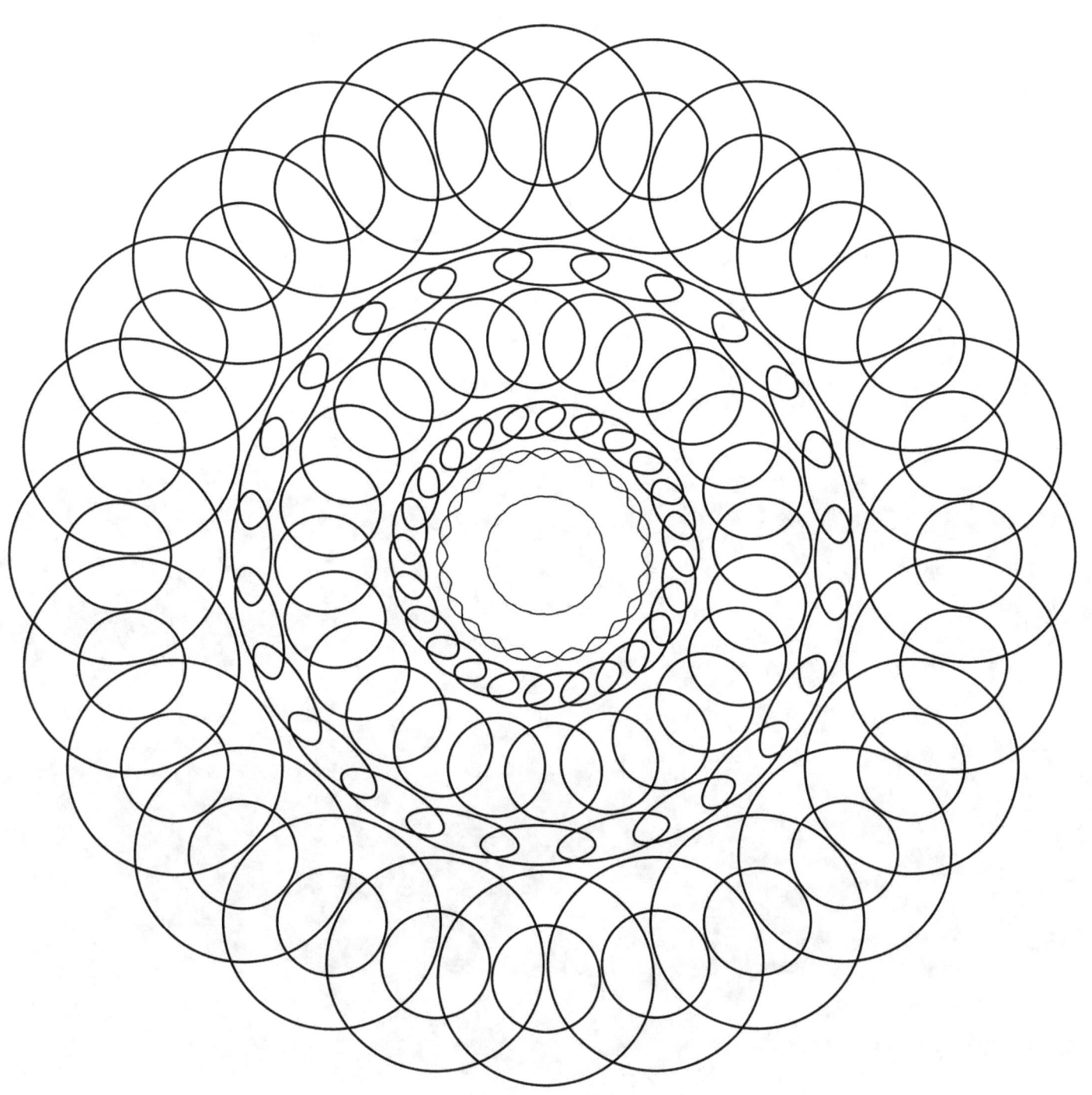

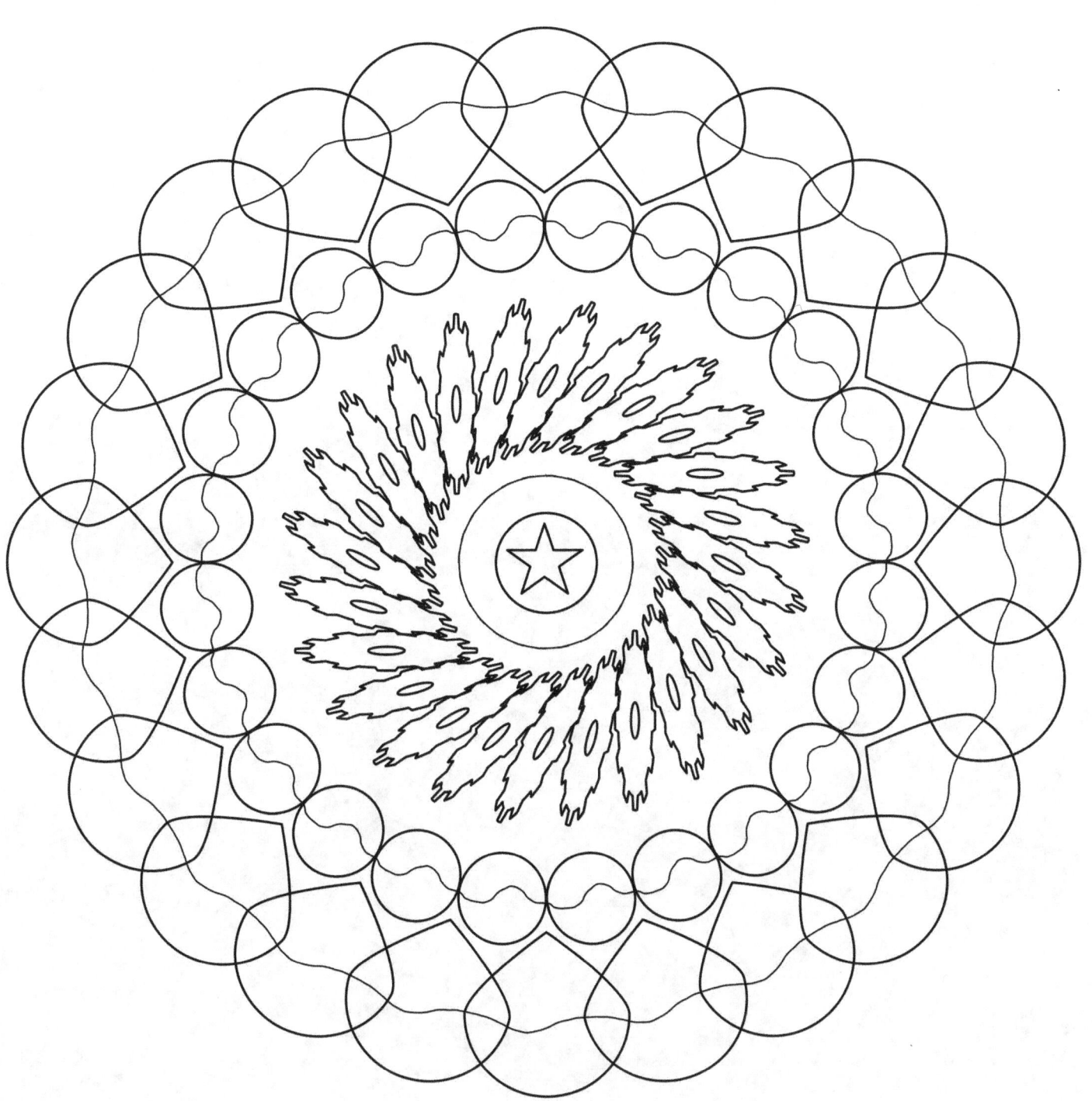

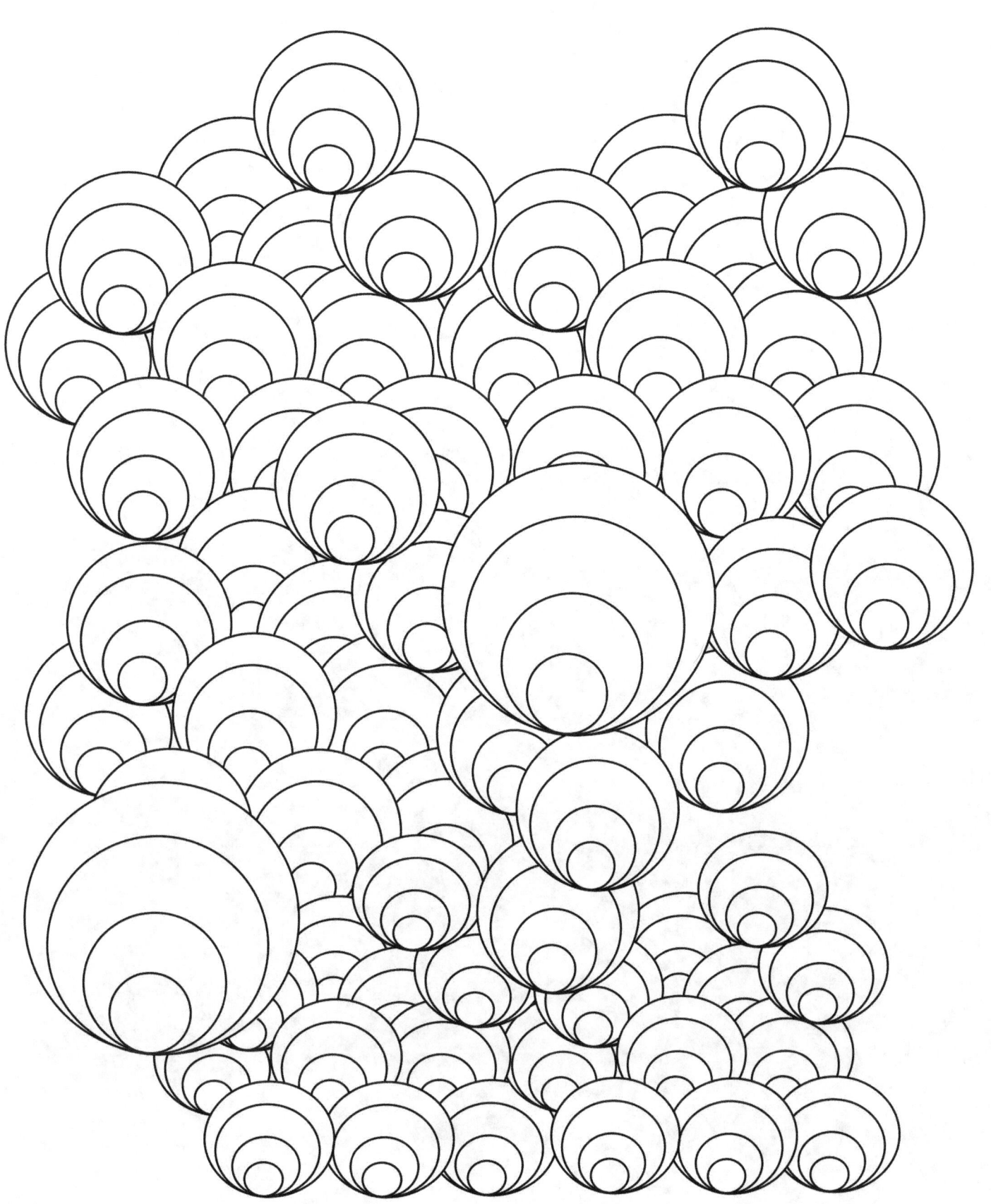

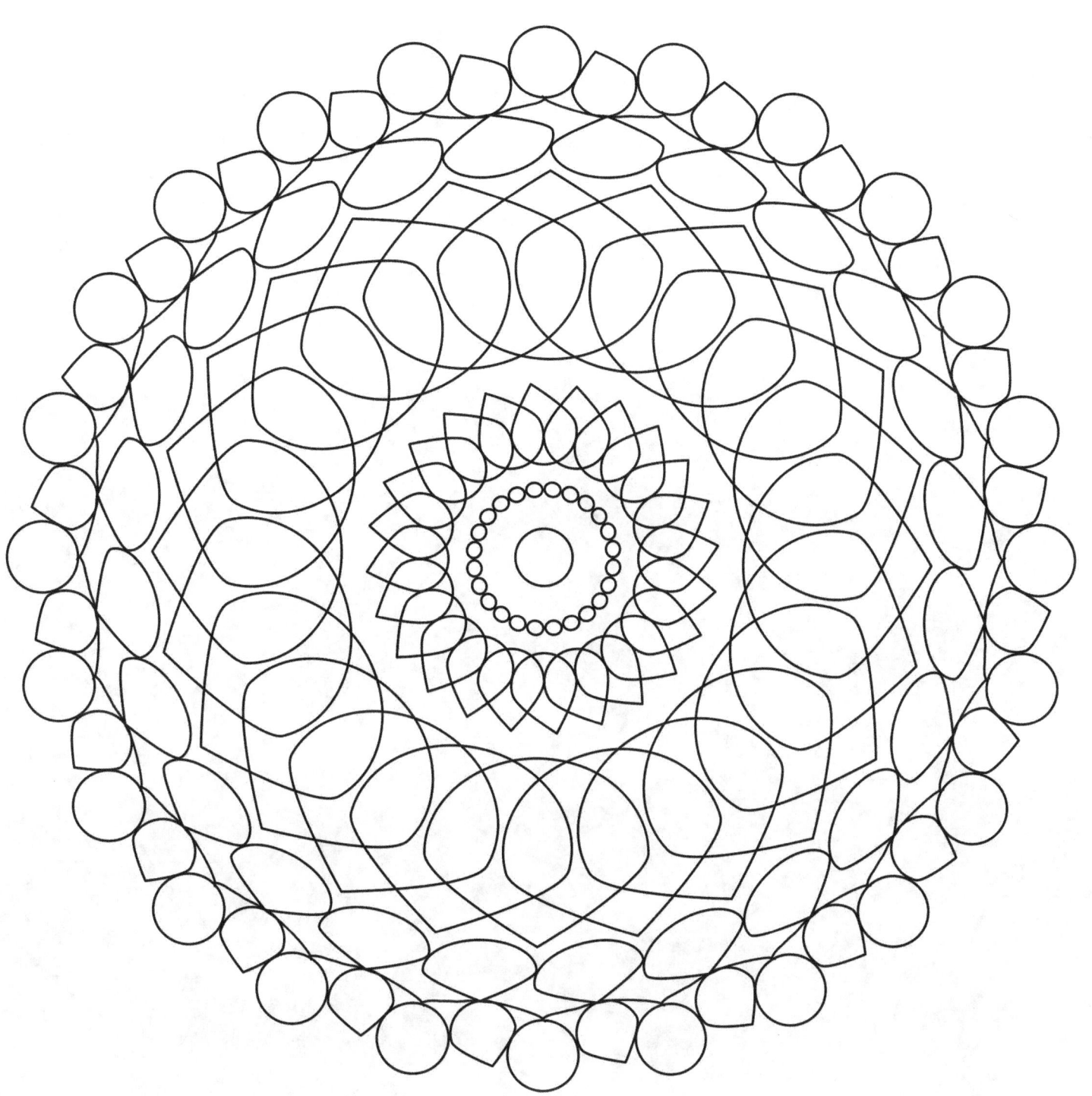

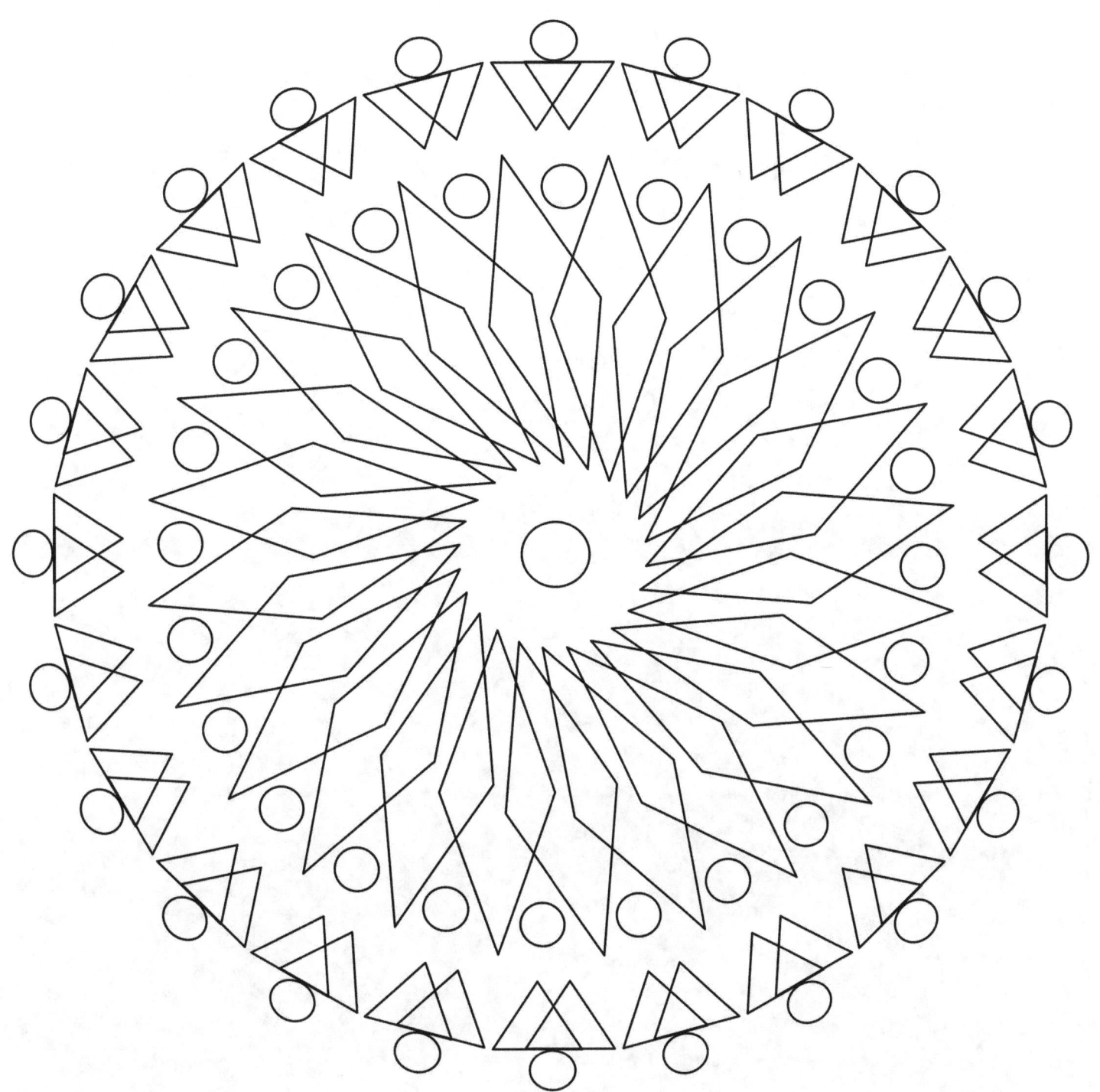

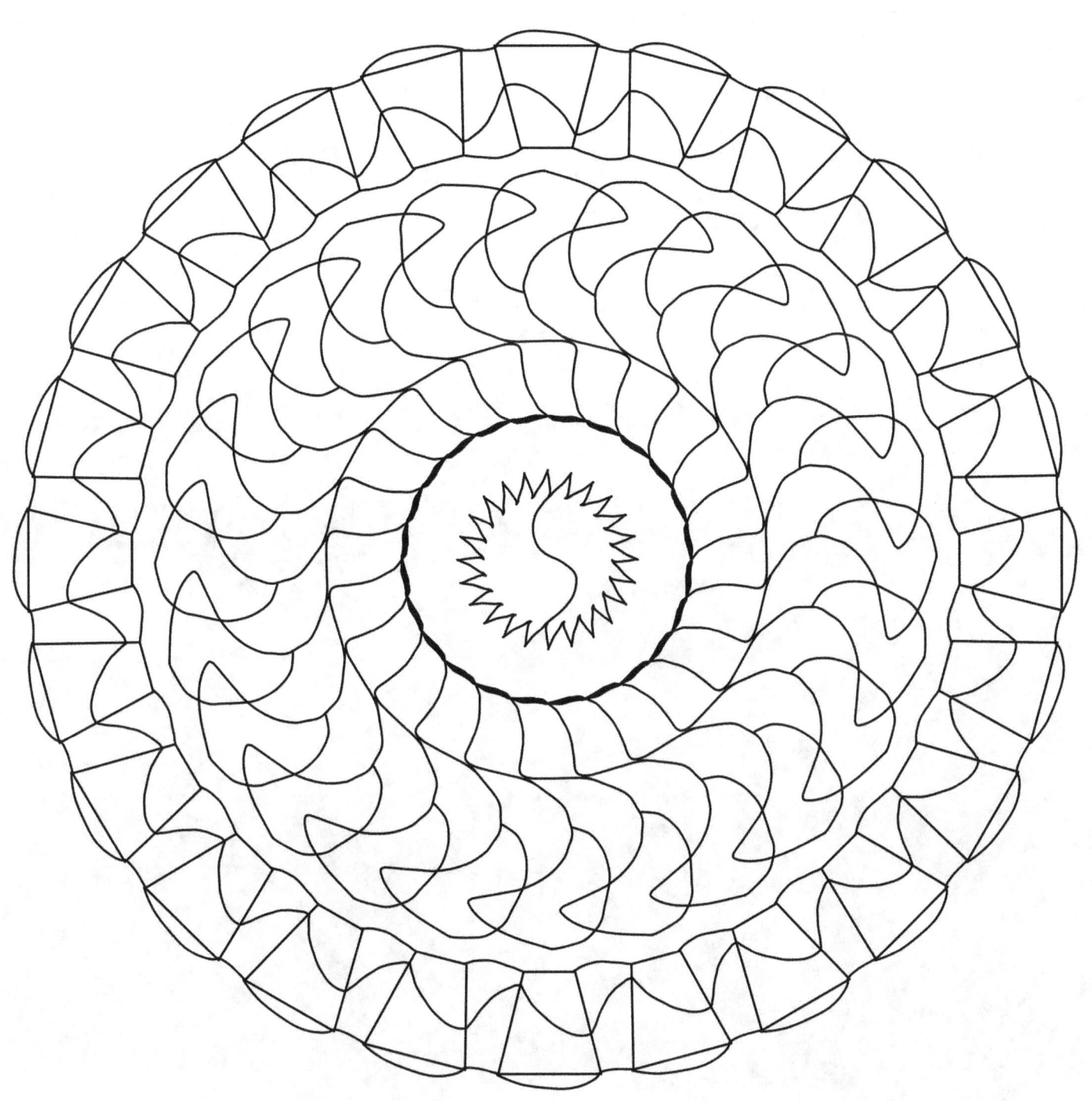

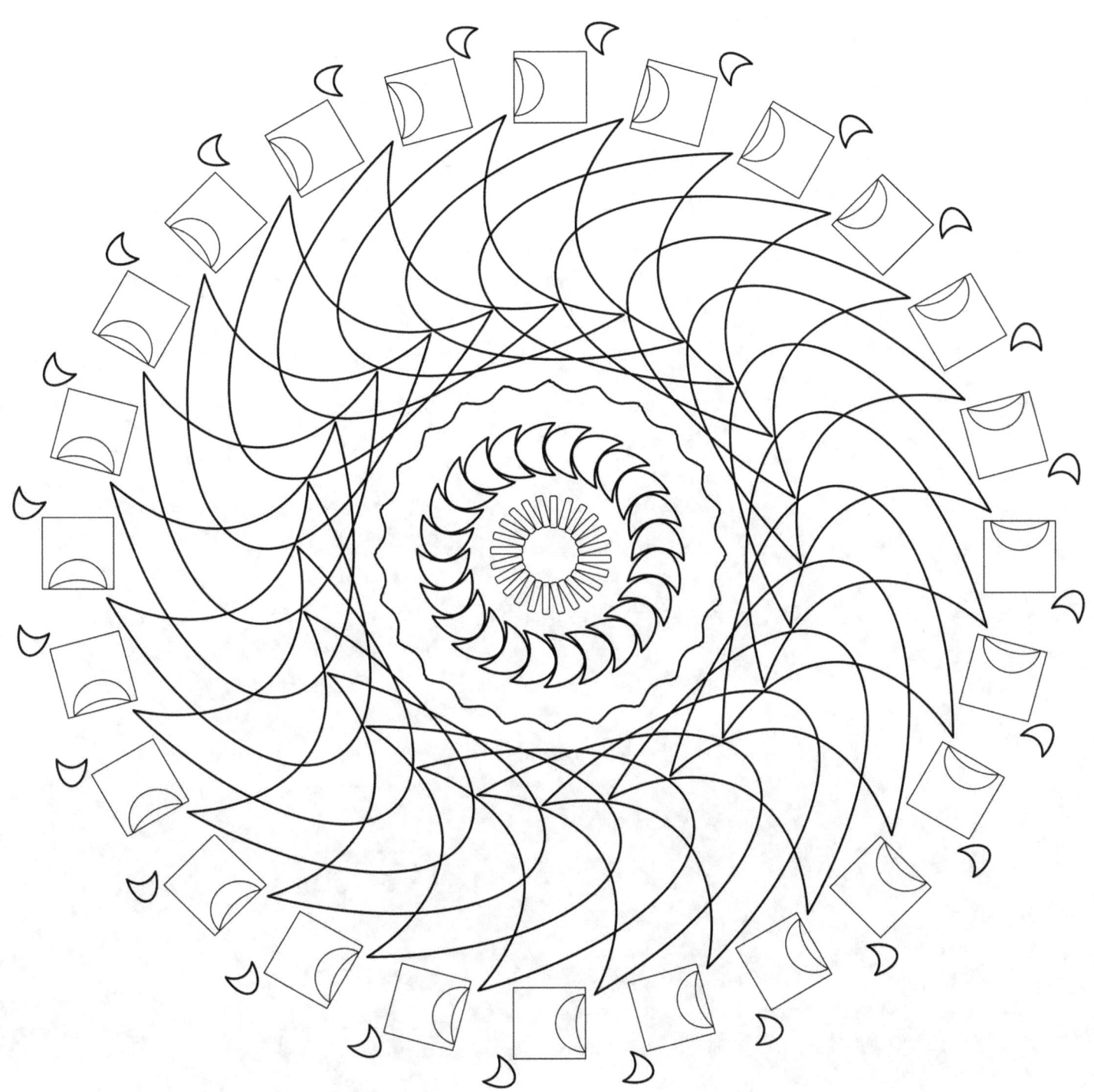

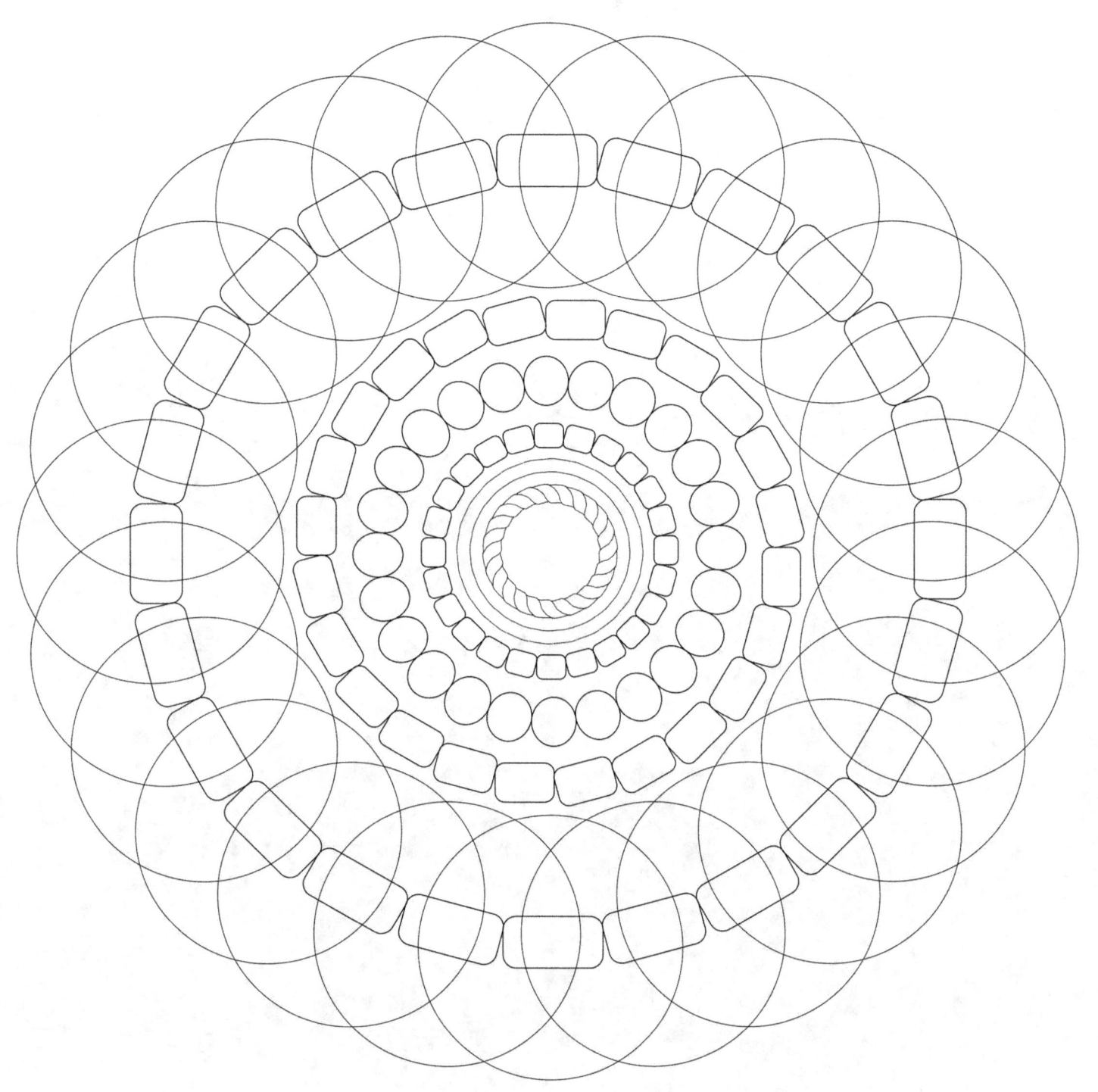

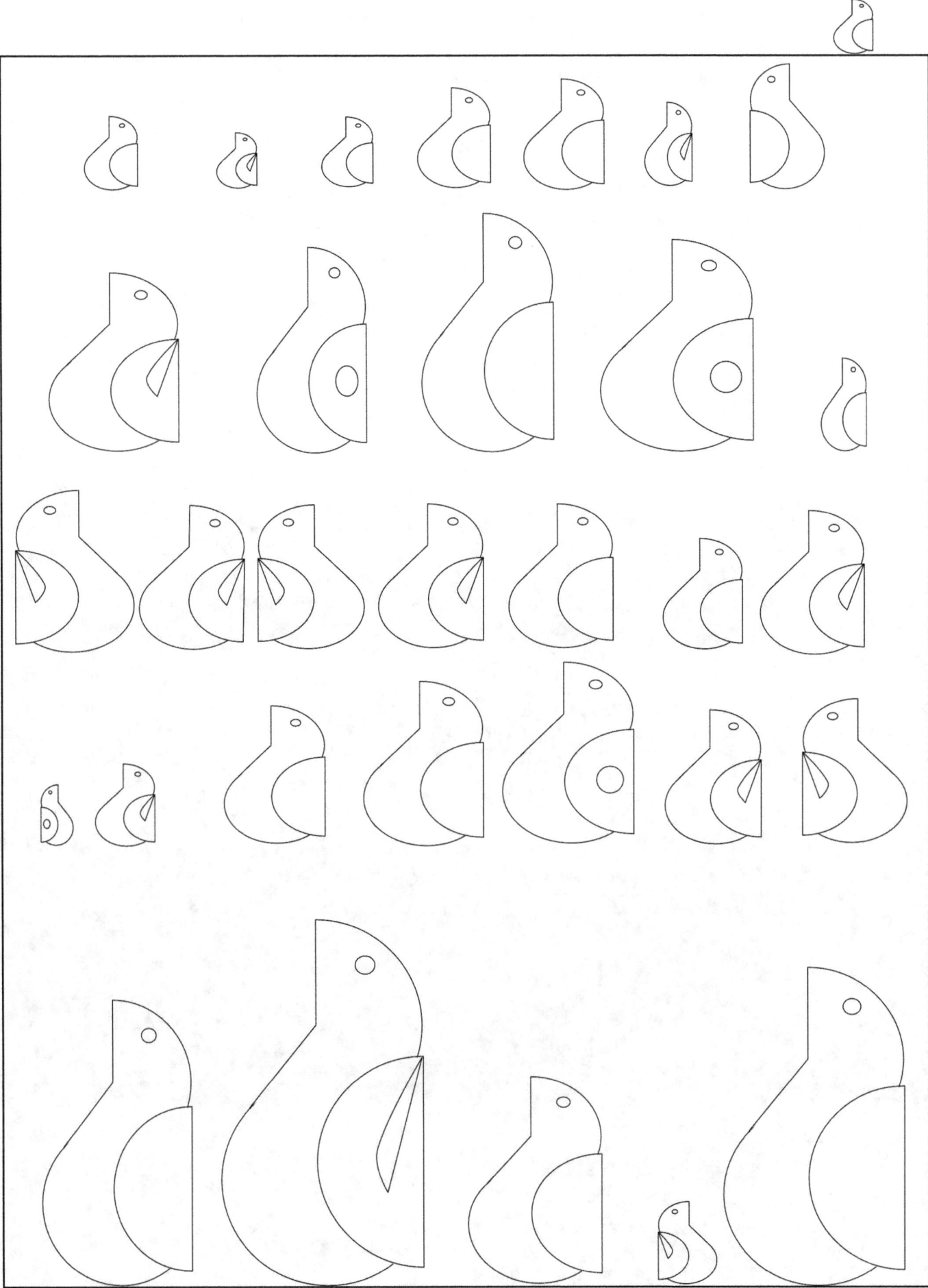

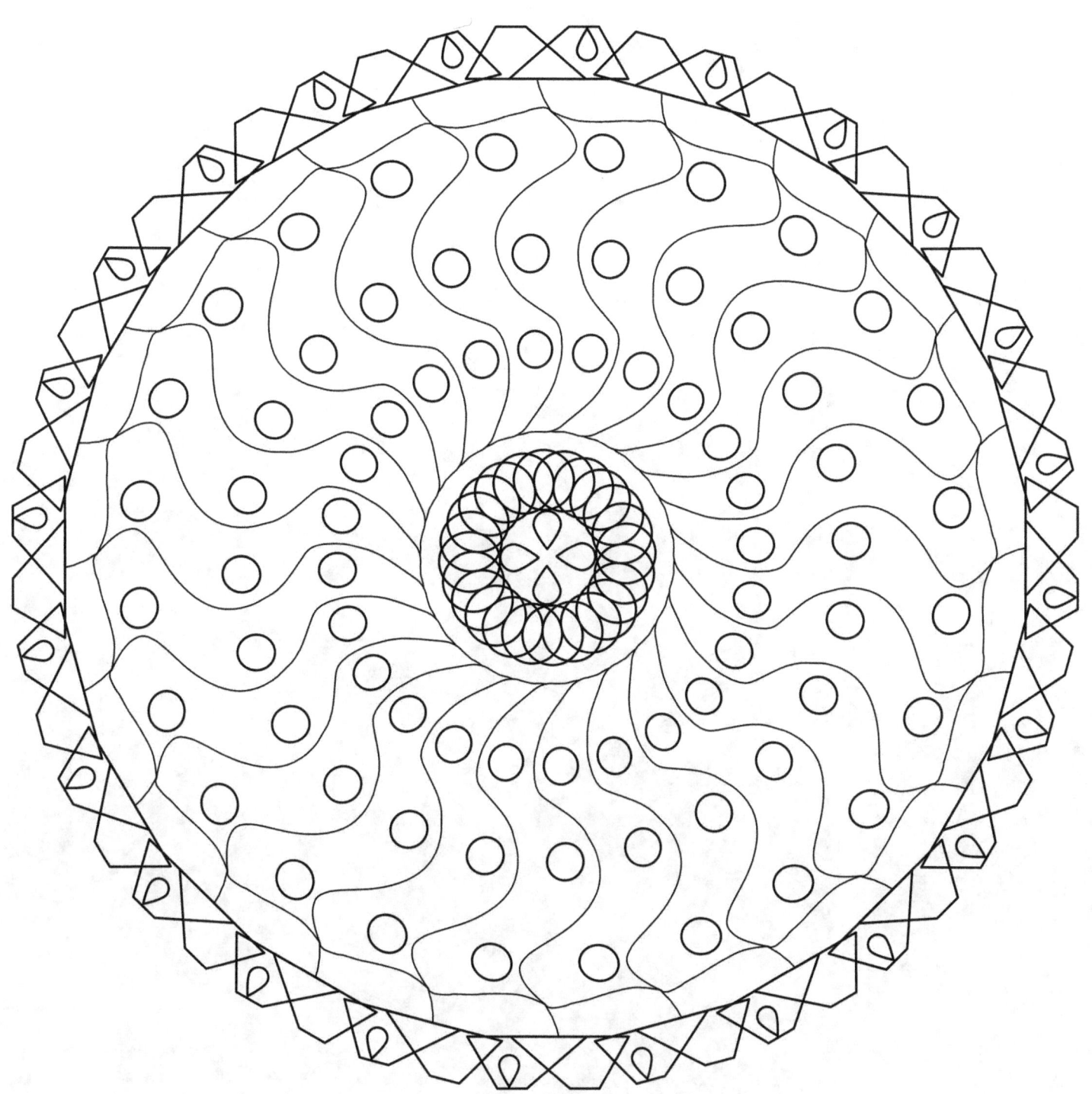

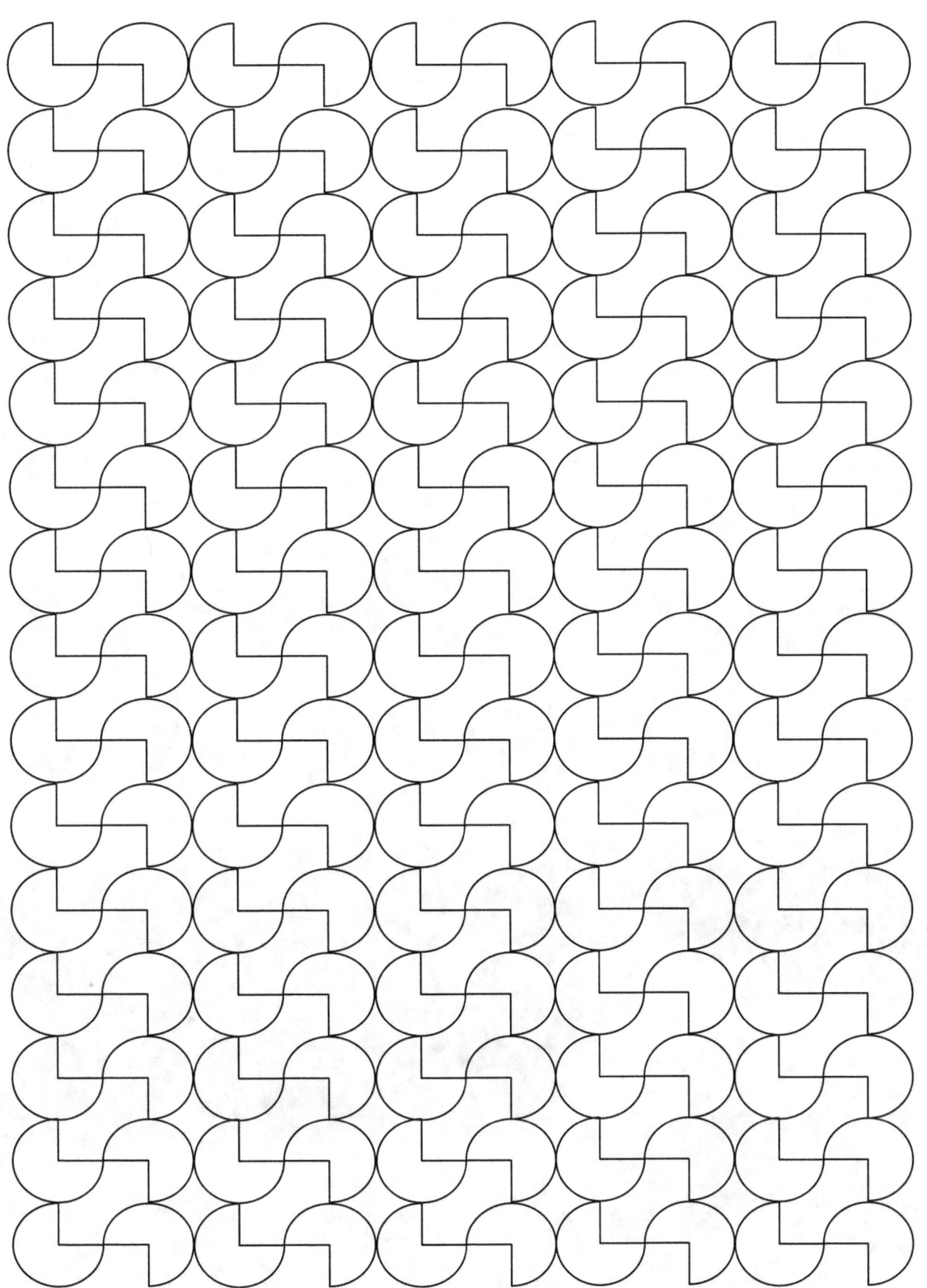

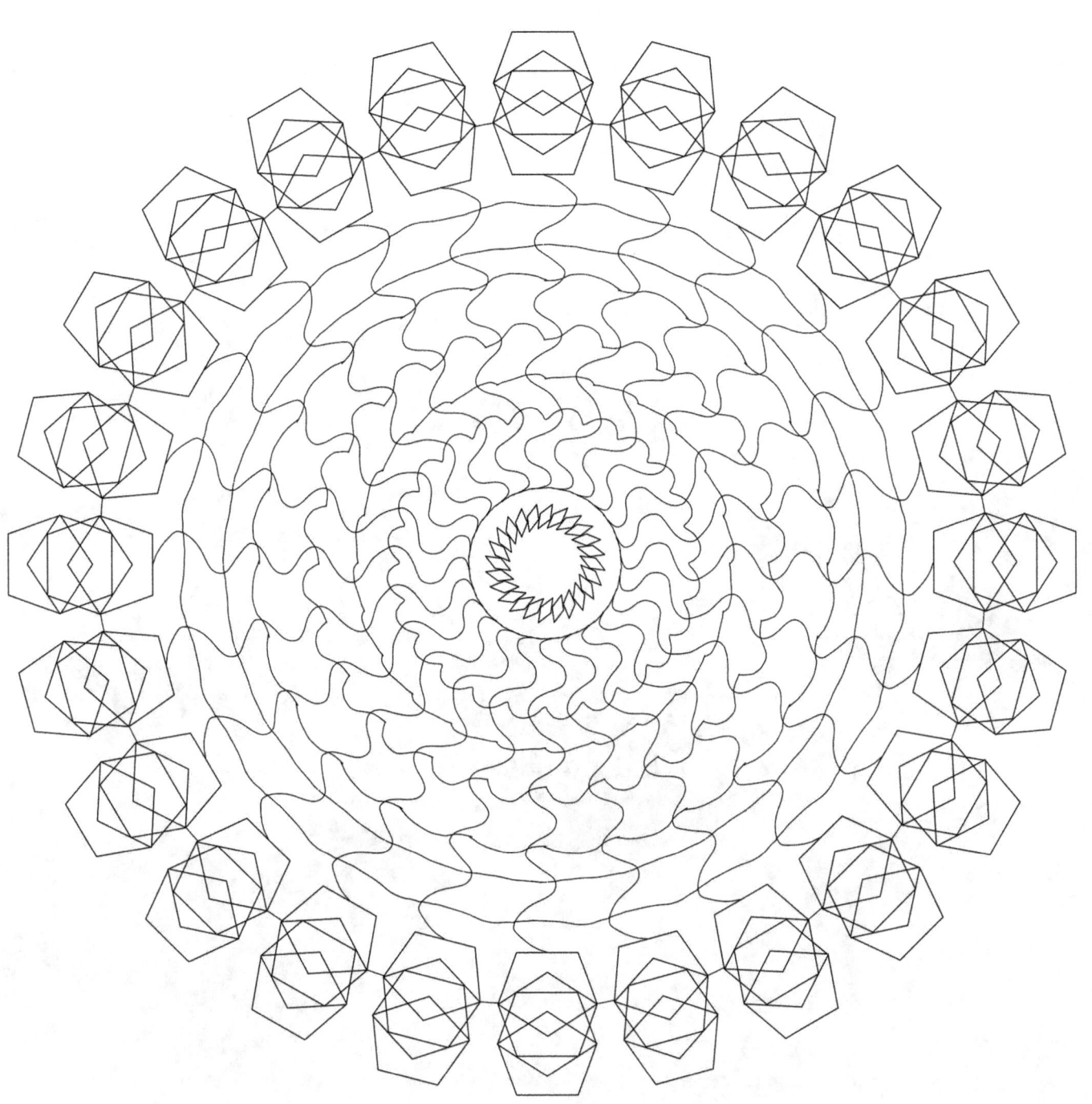

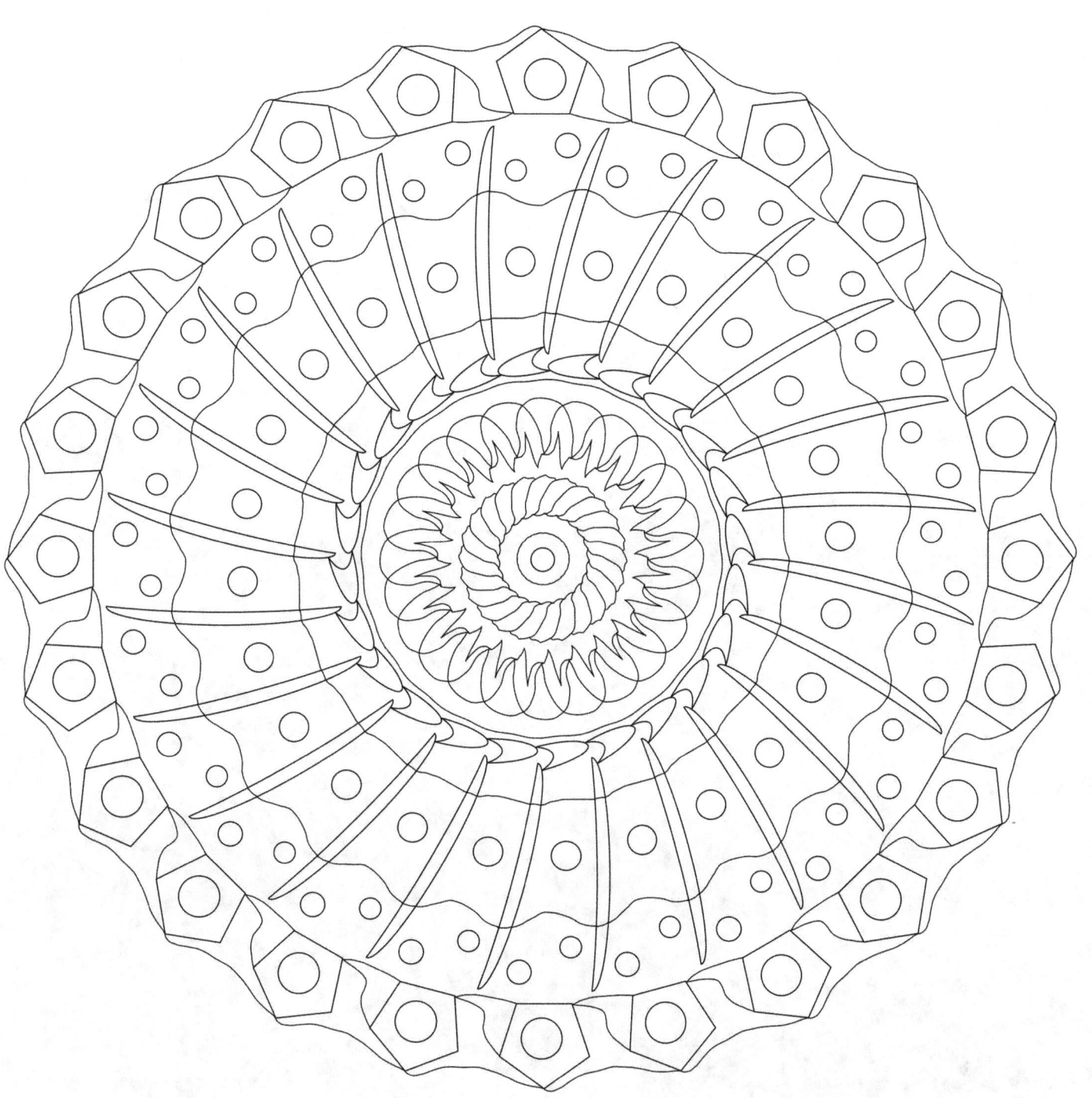

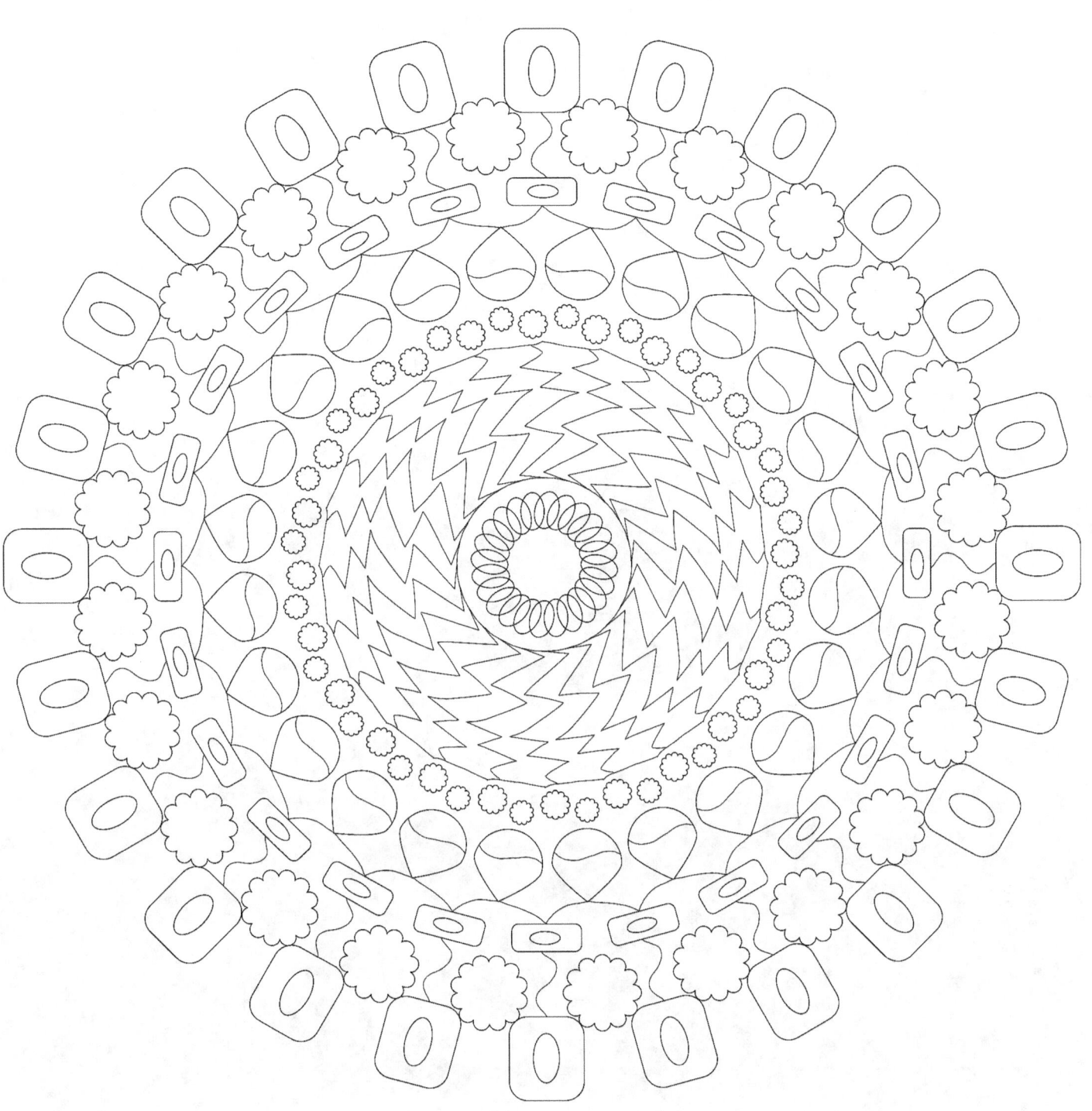

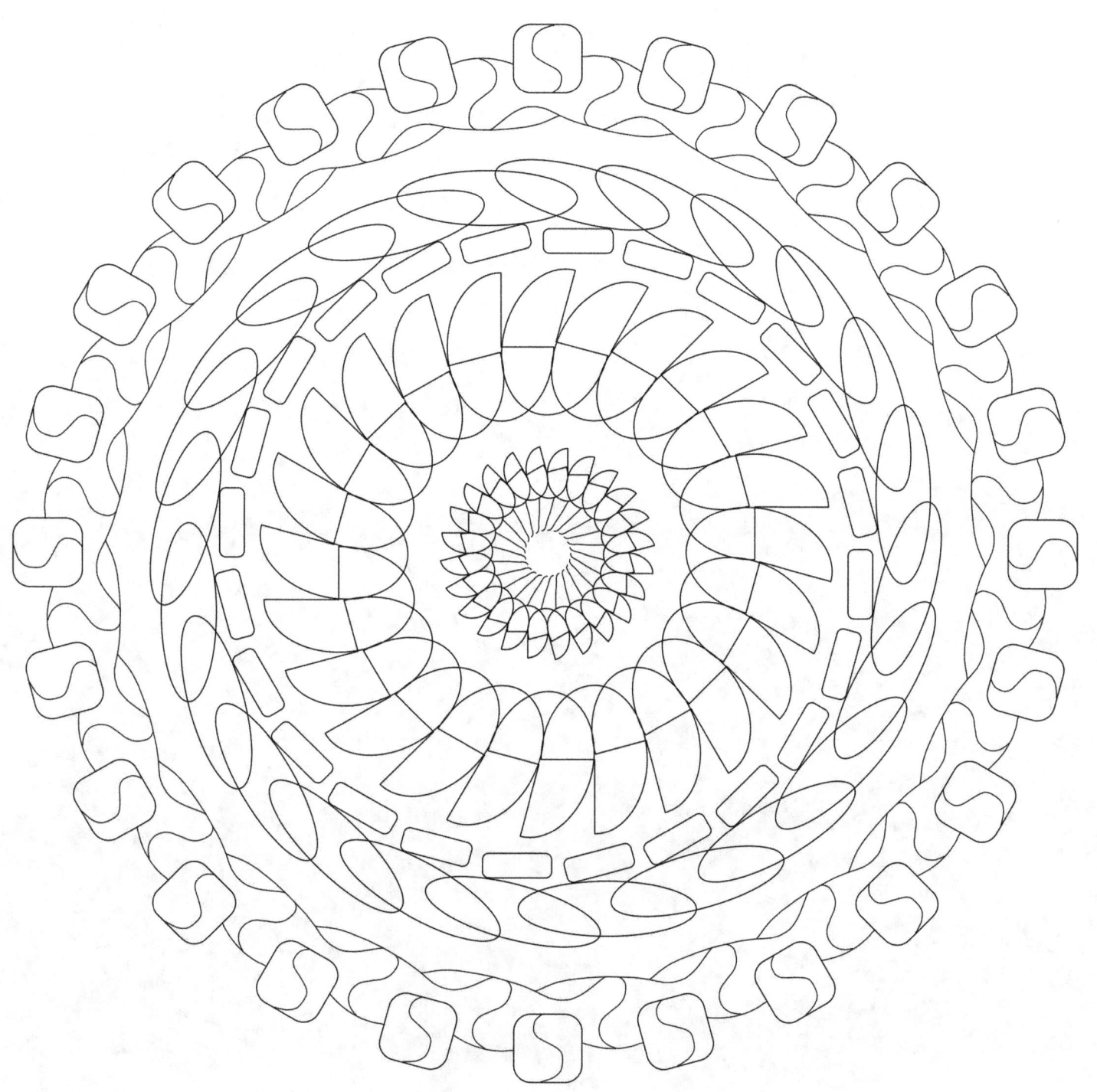

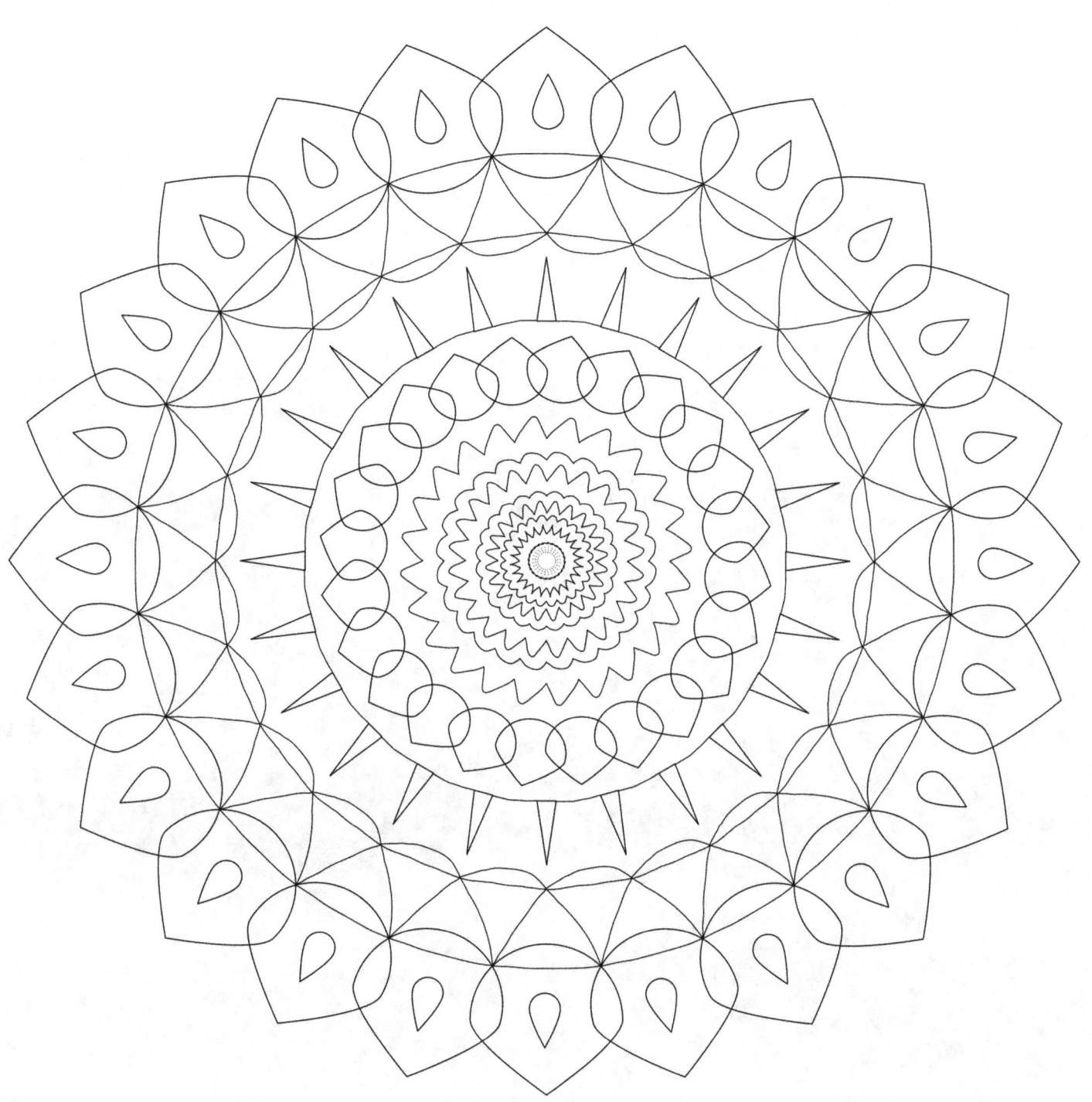

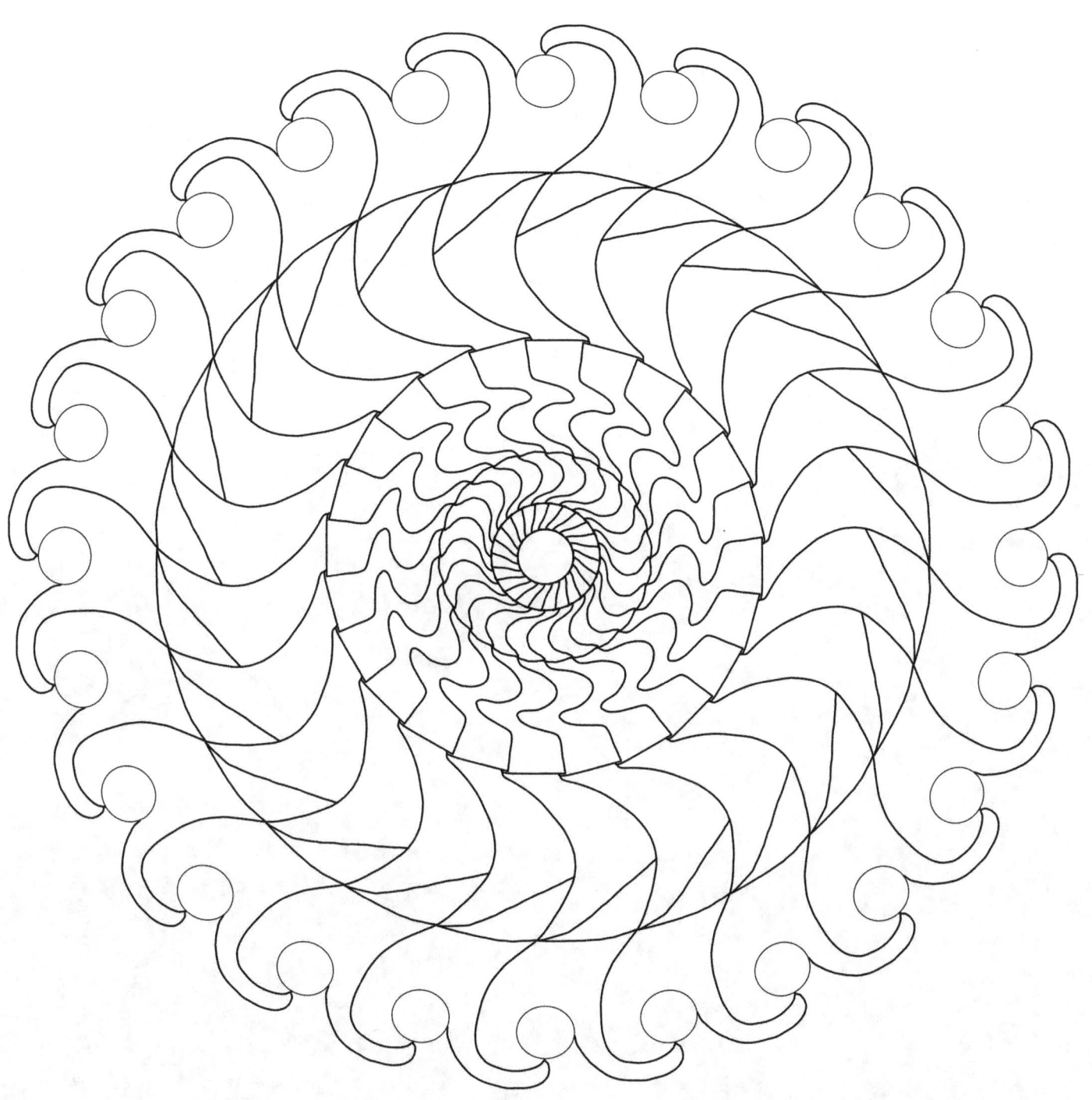

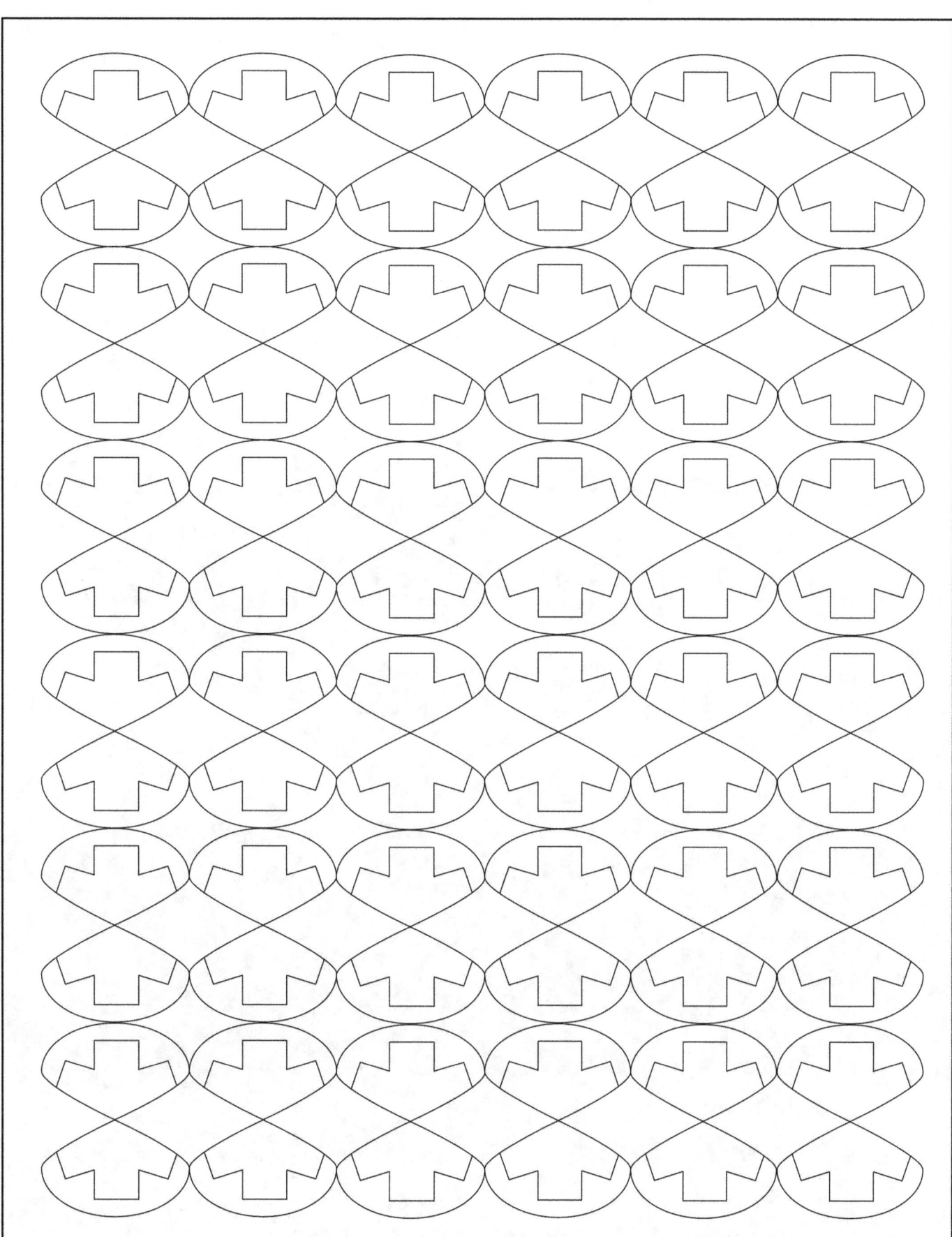

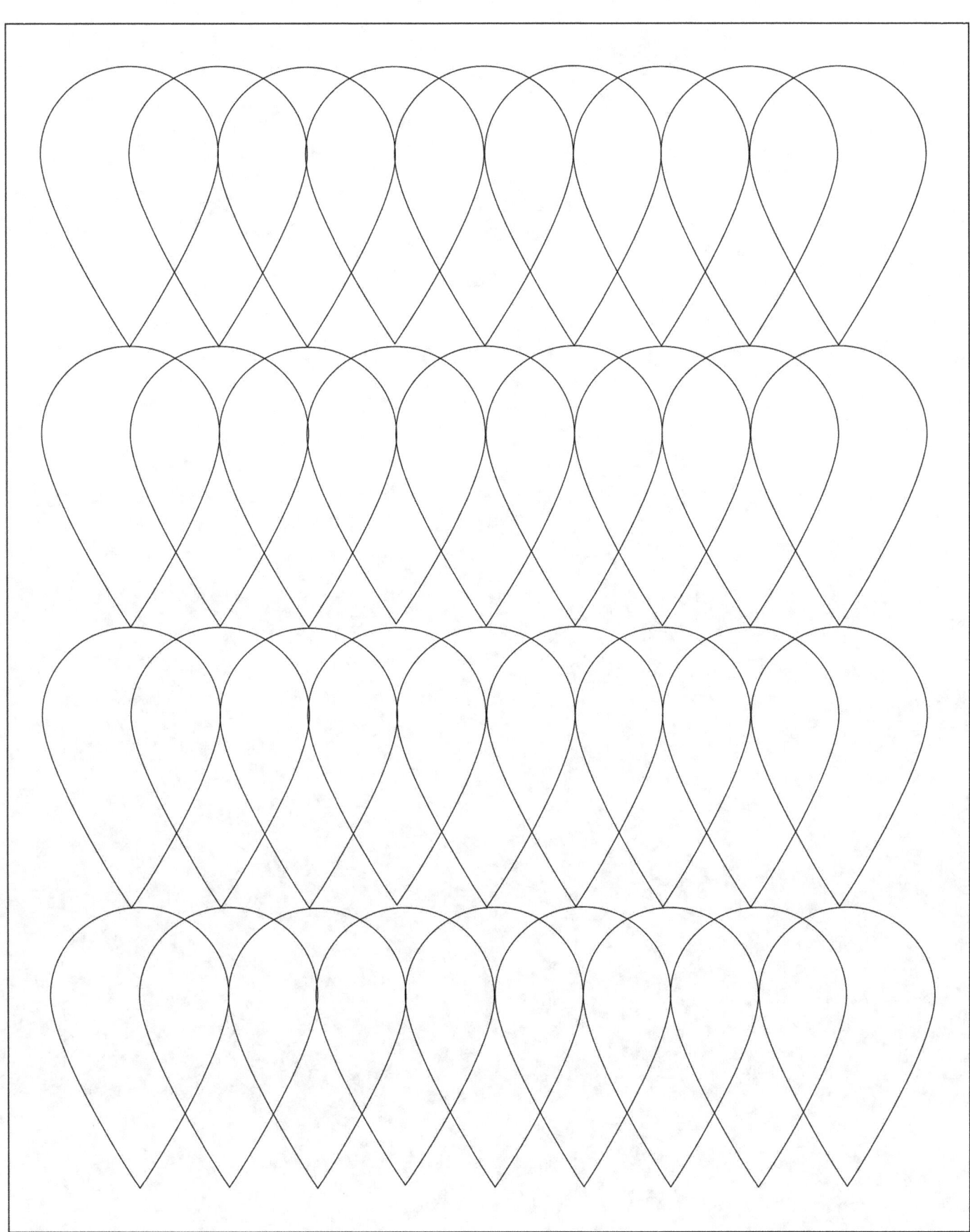

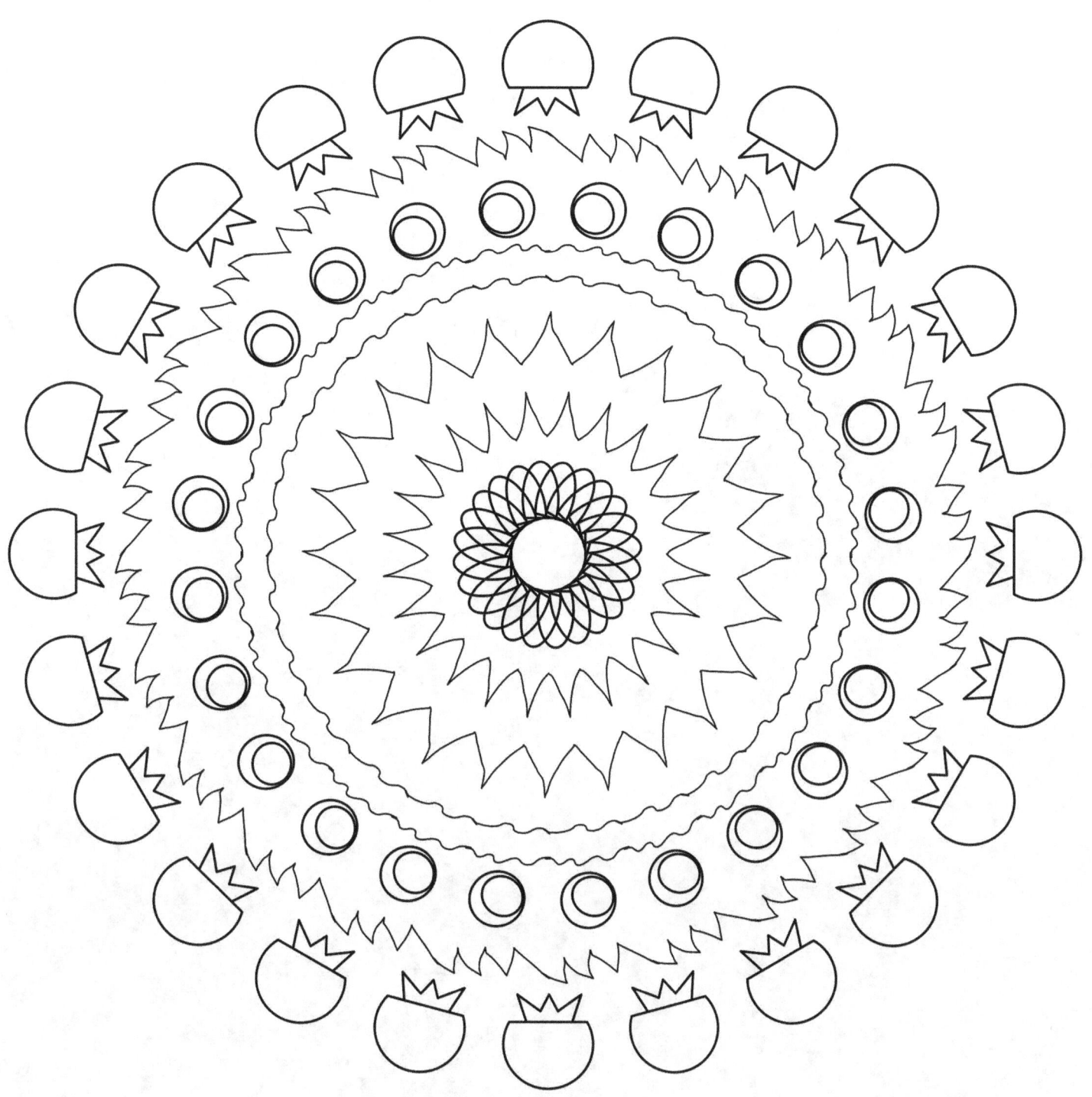

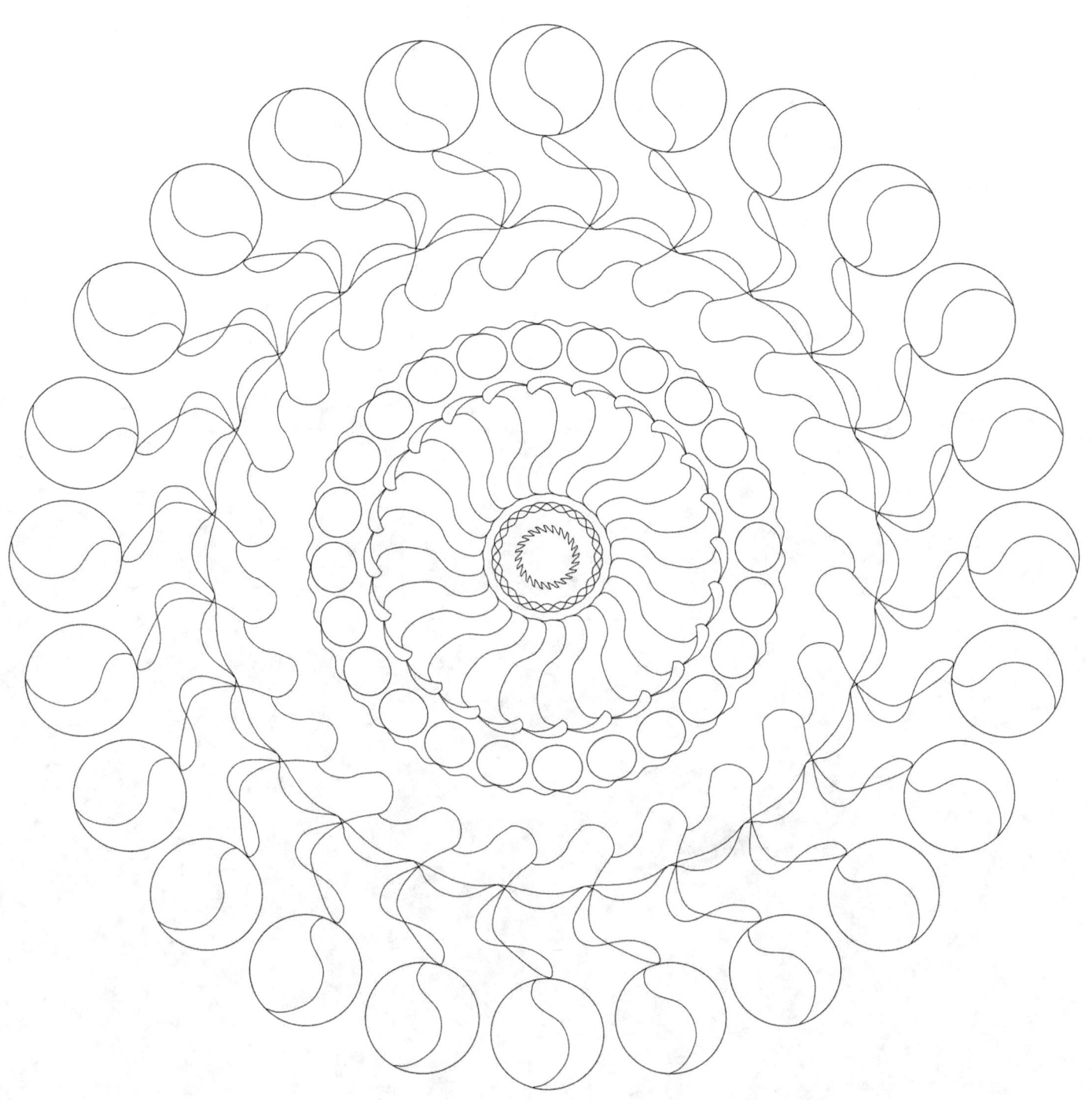

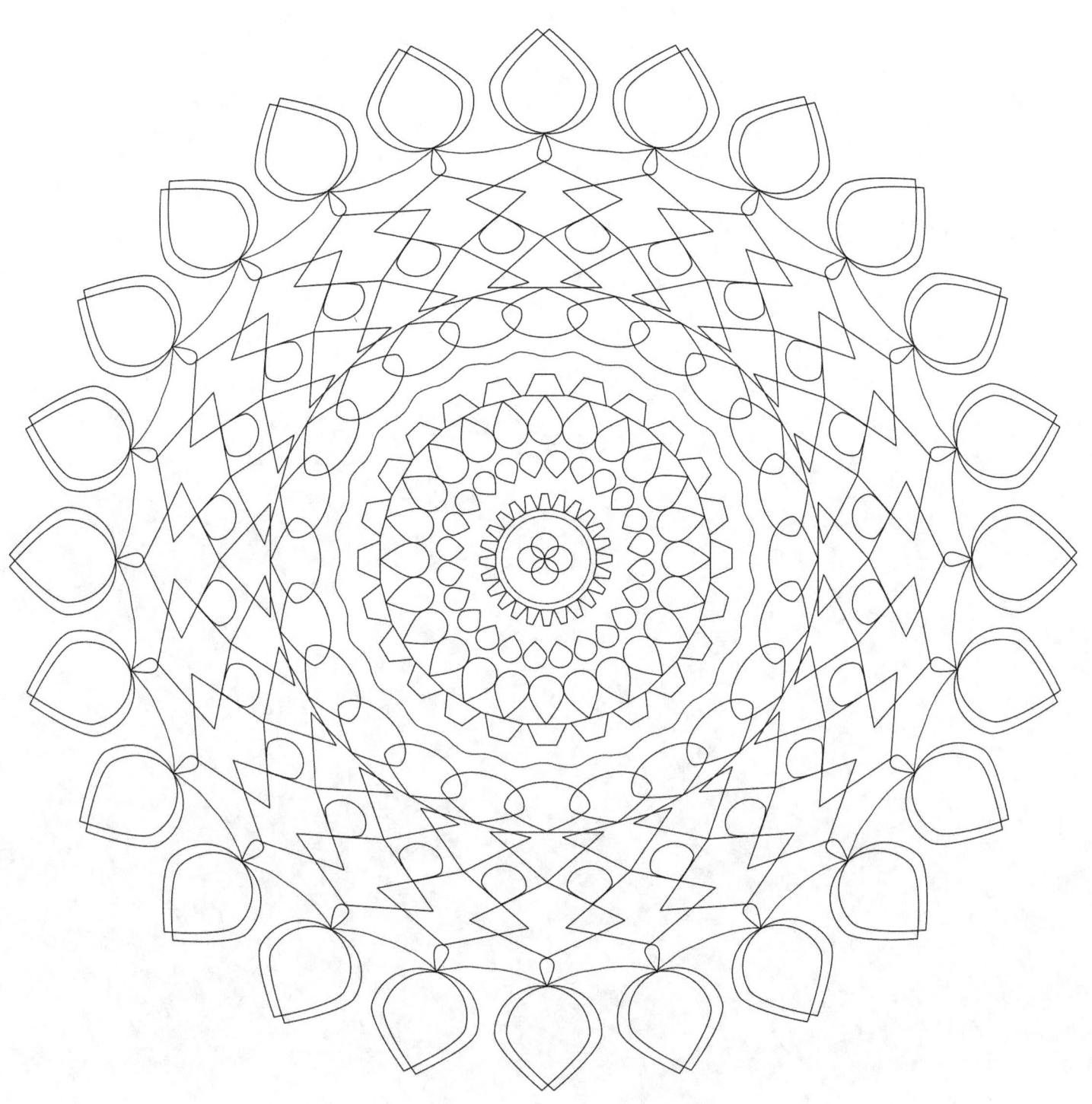

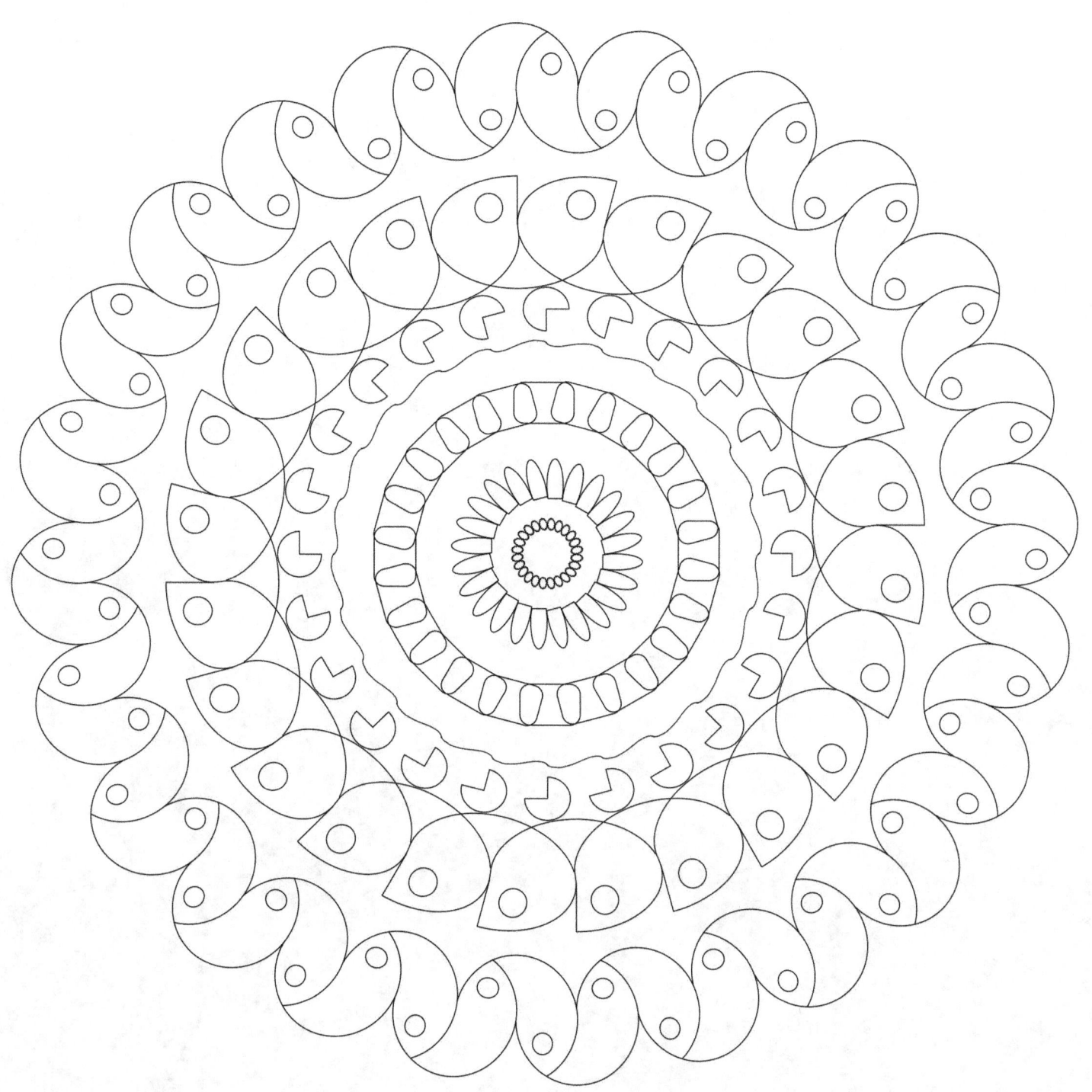

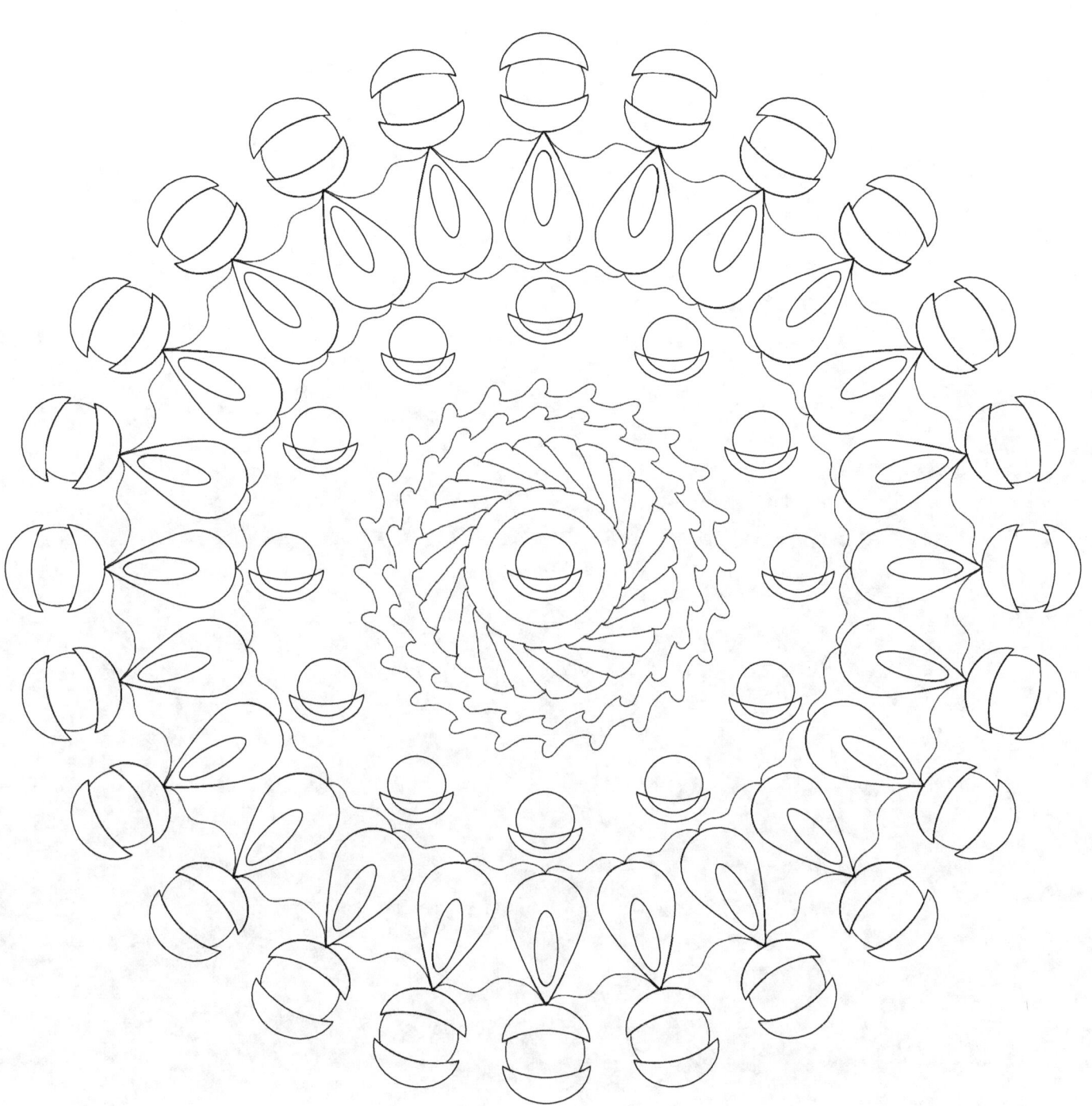

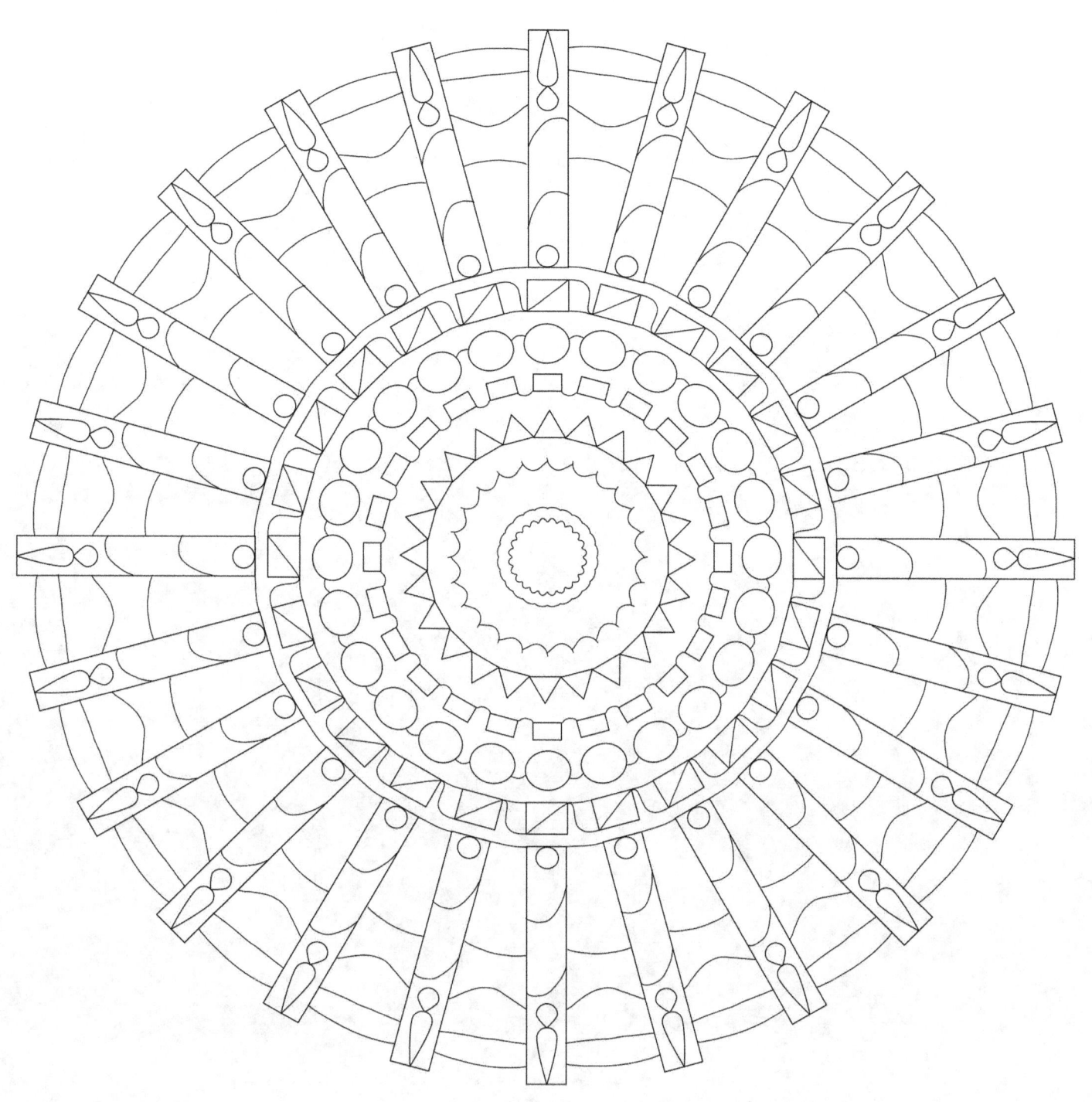

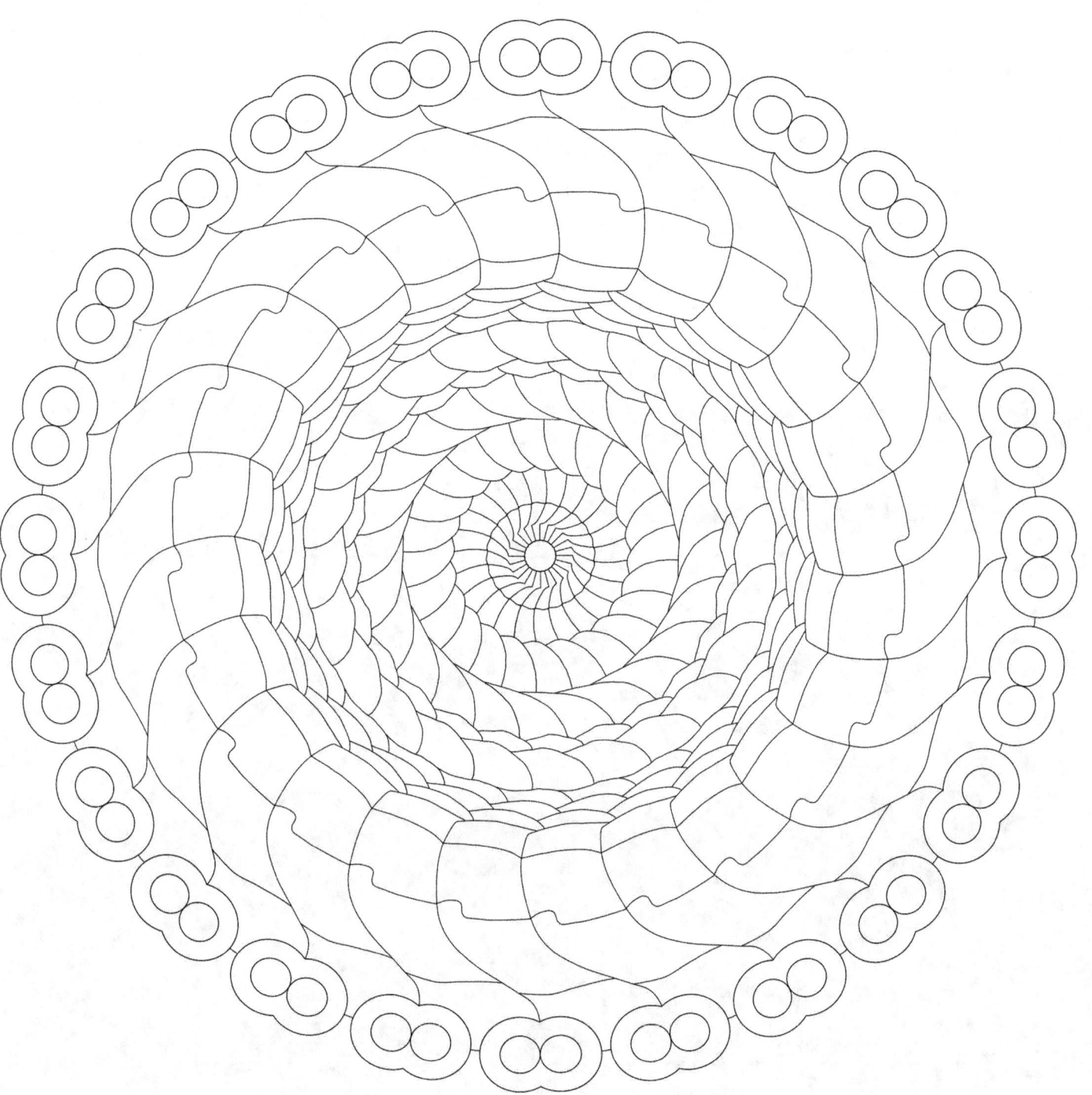

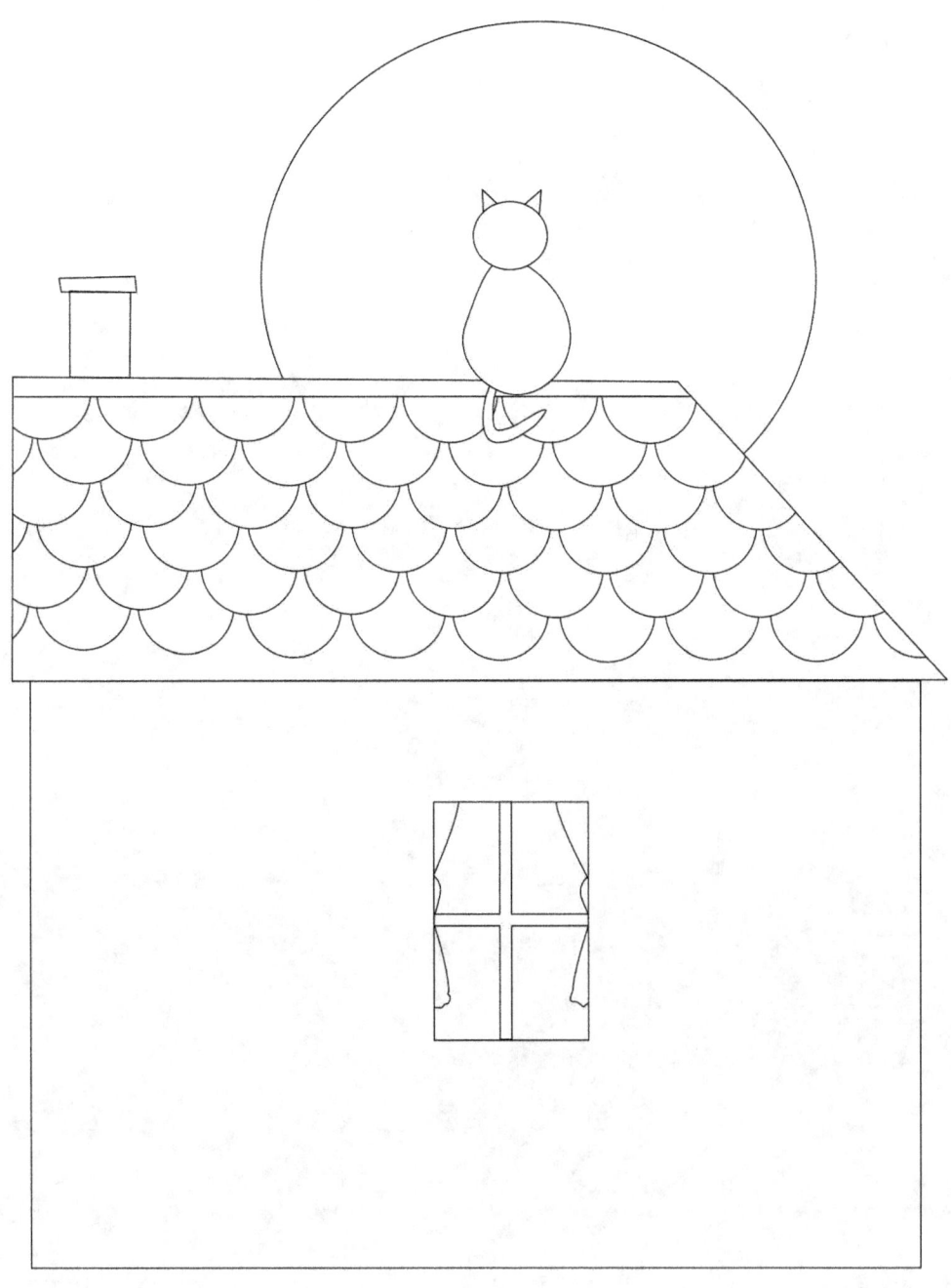

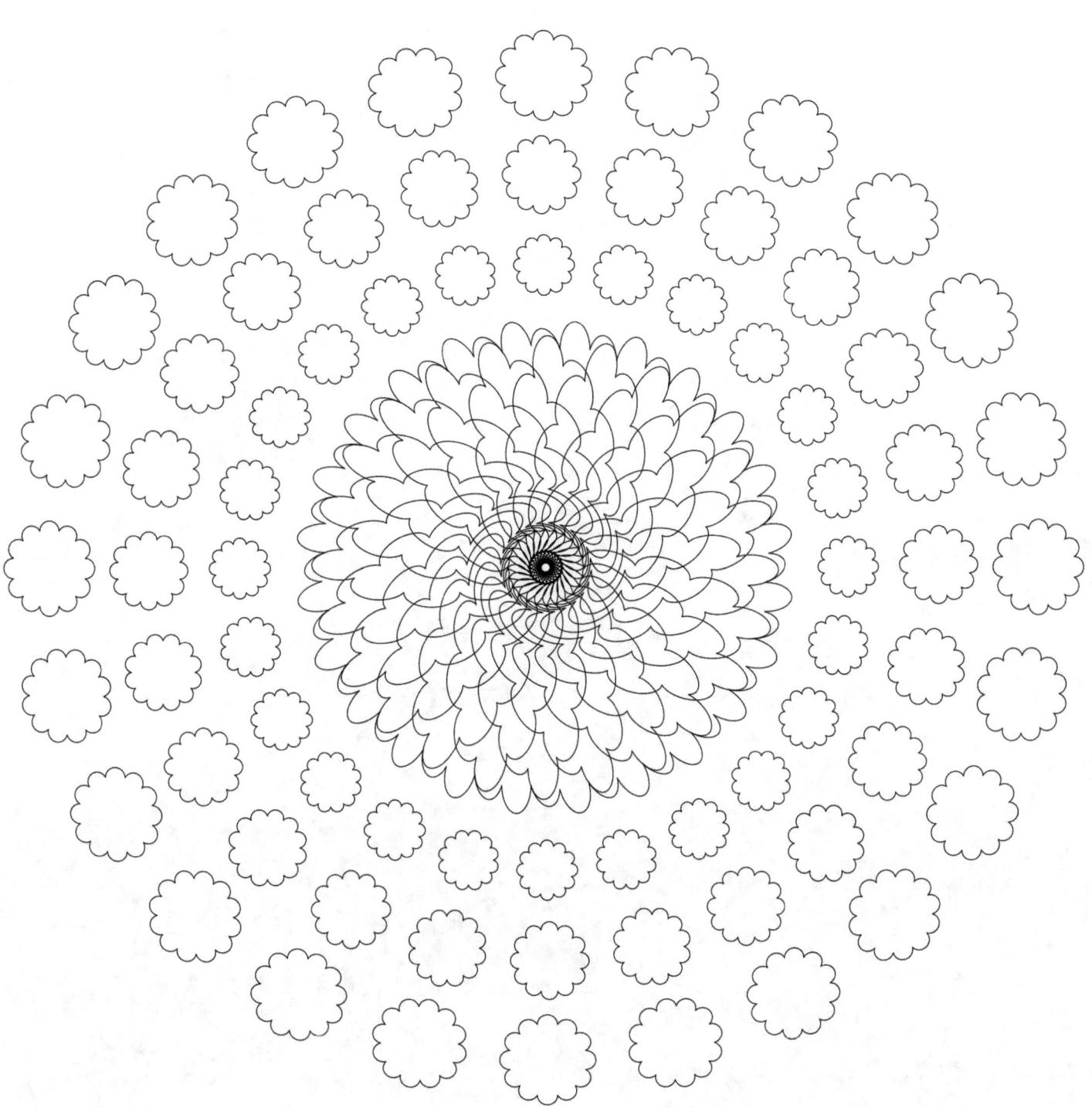

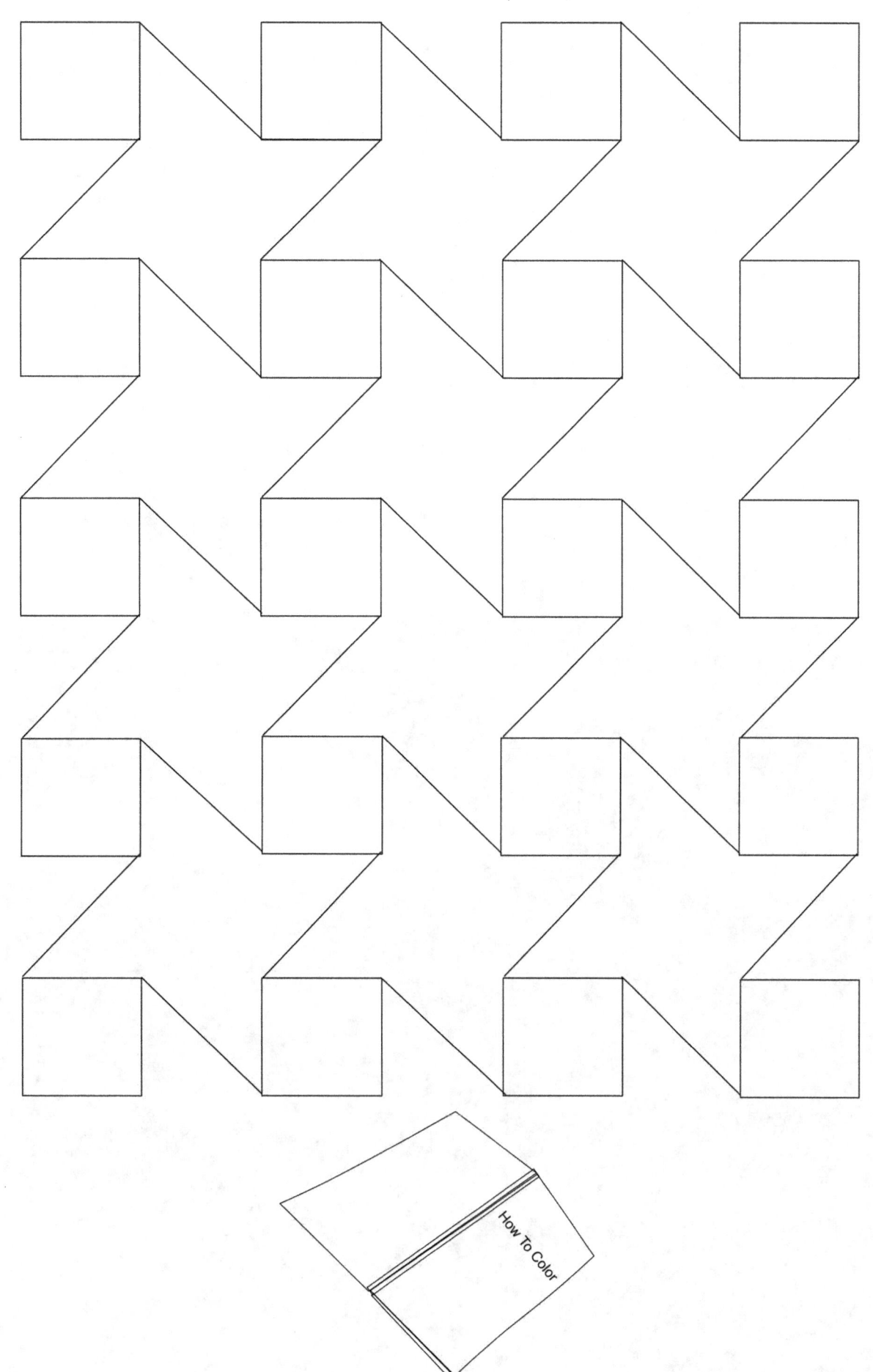

How To Color

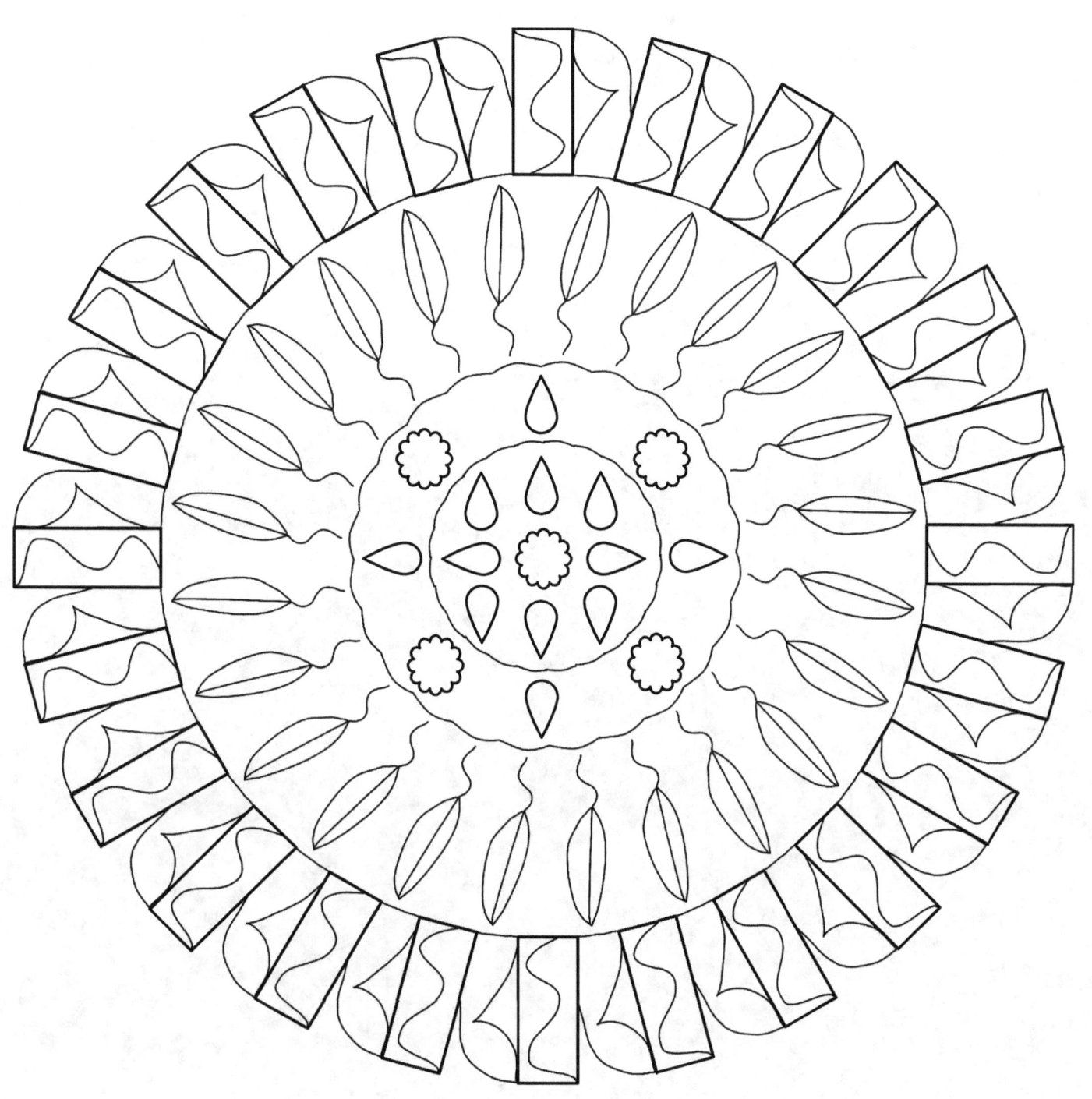

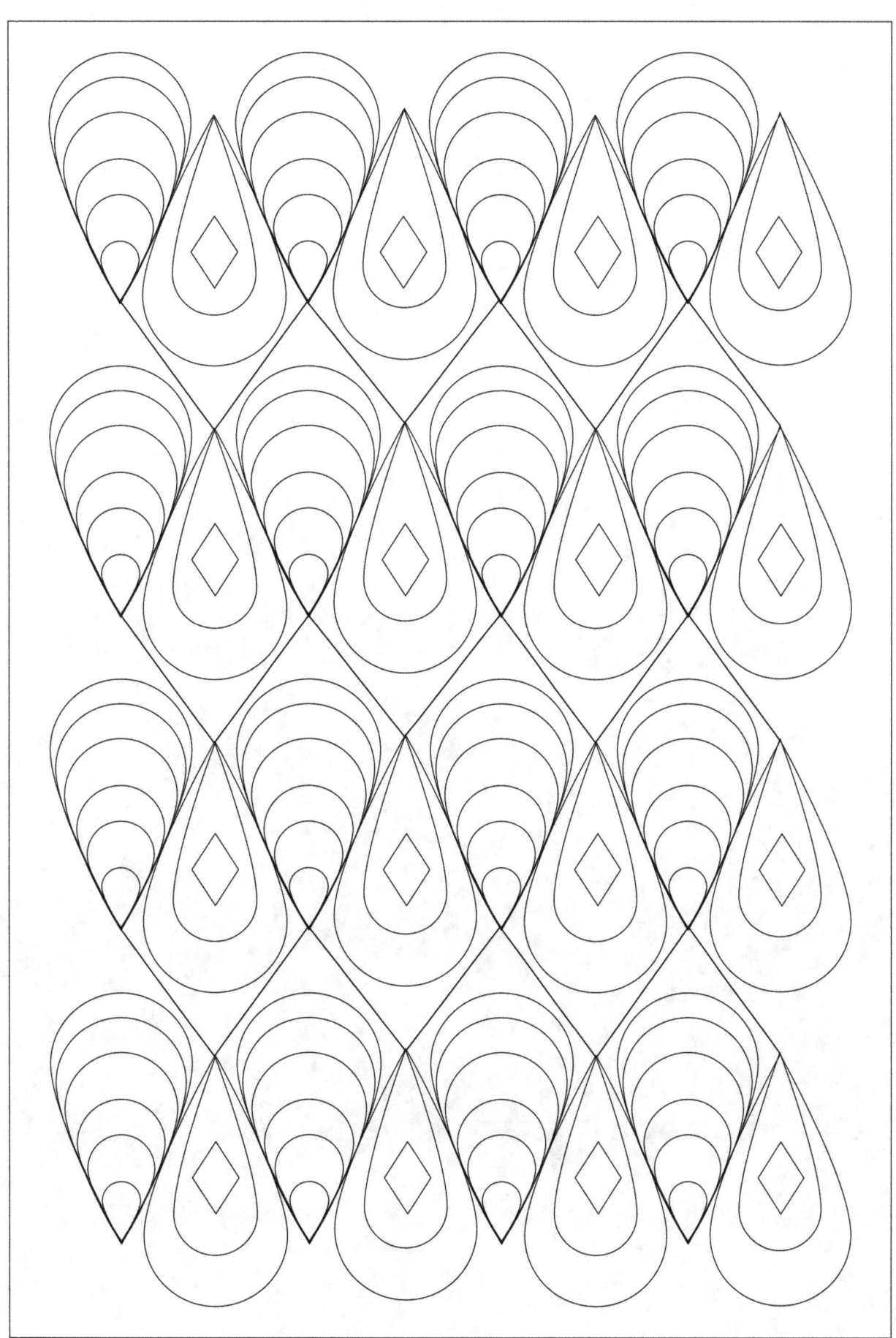

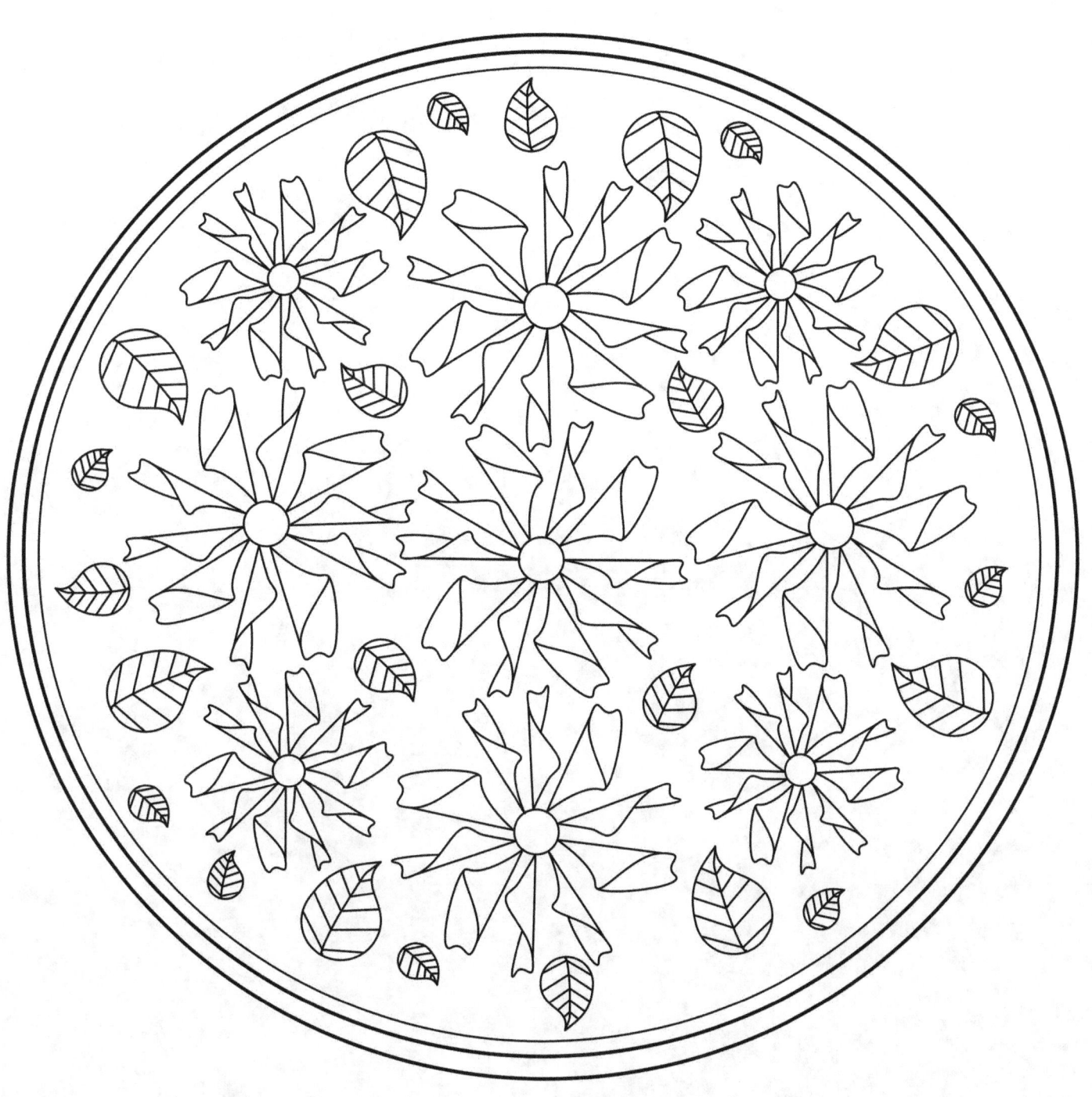

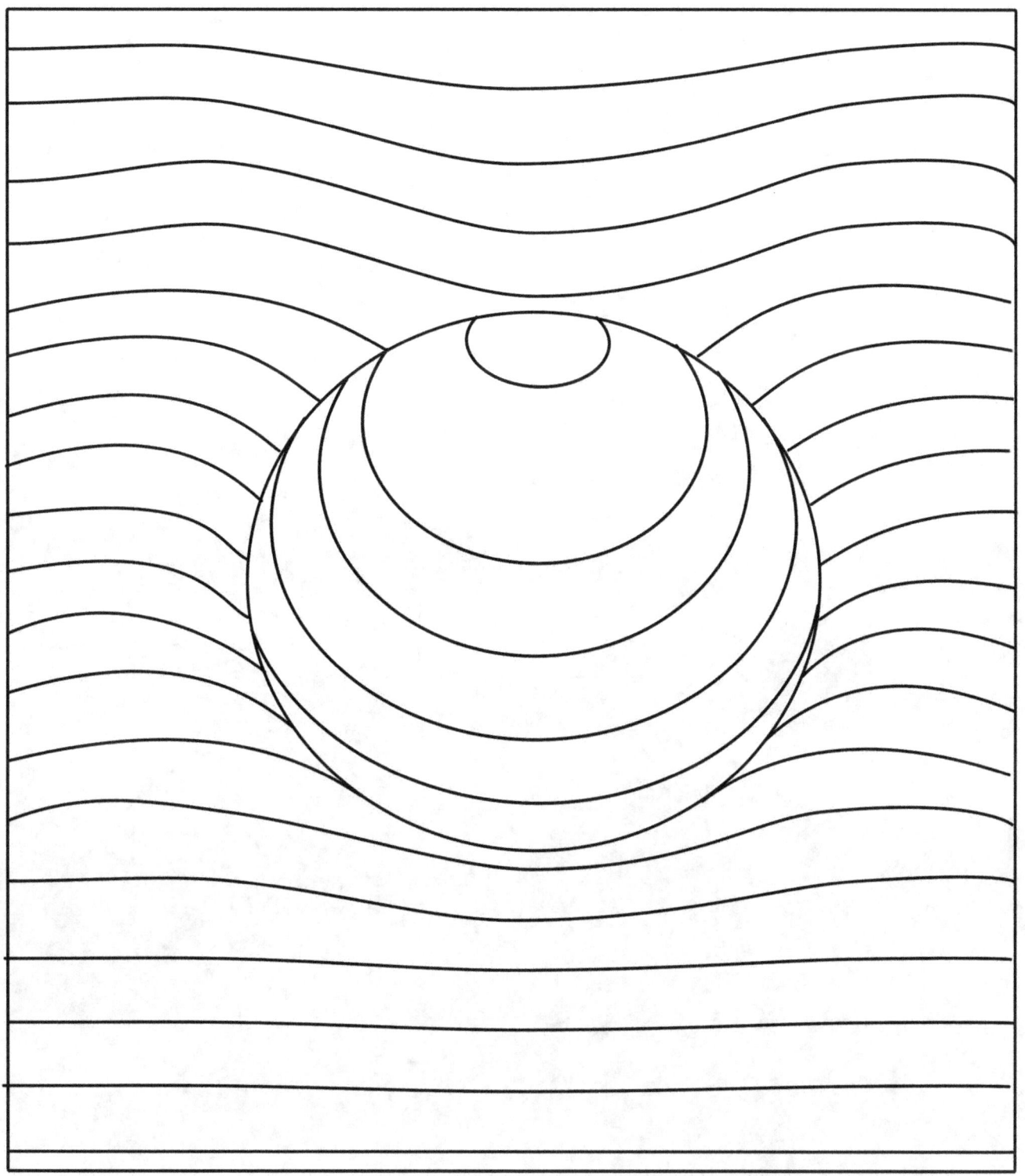

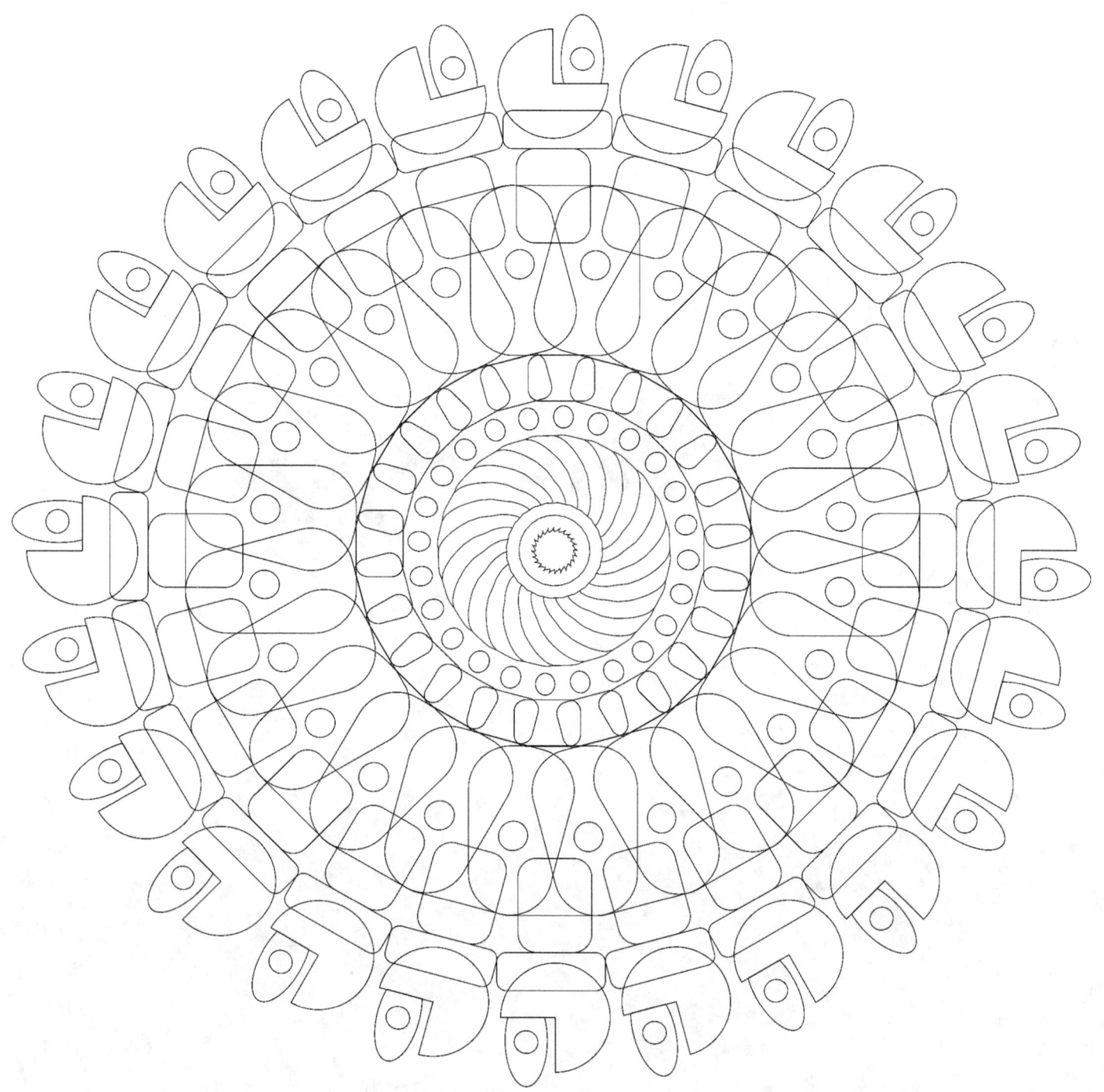

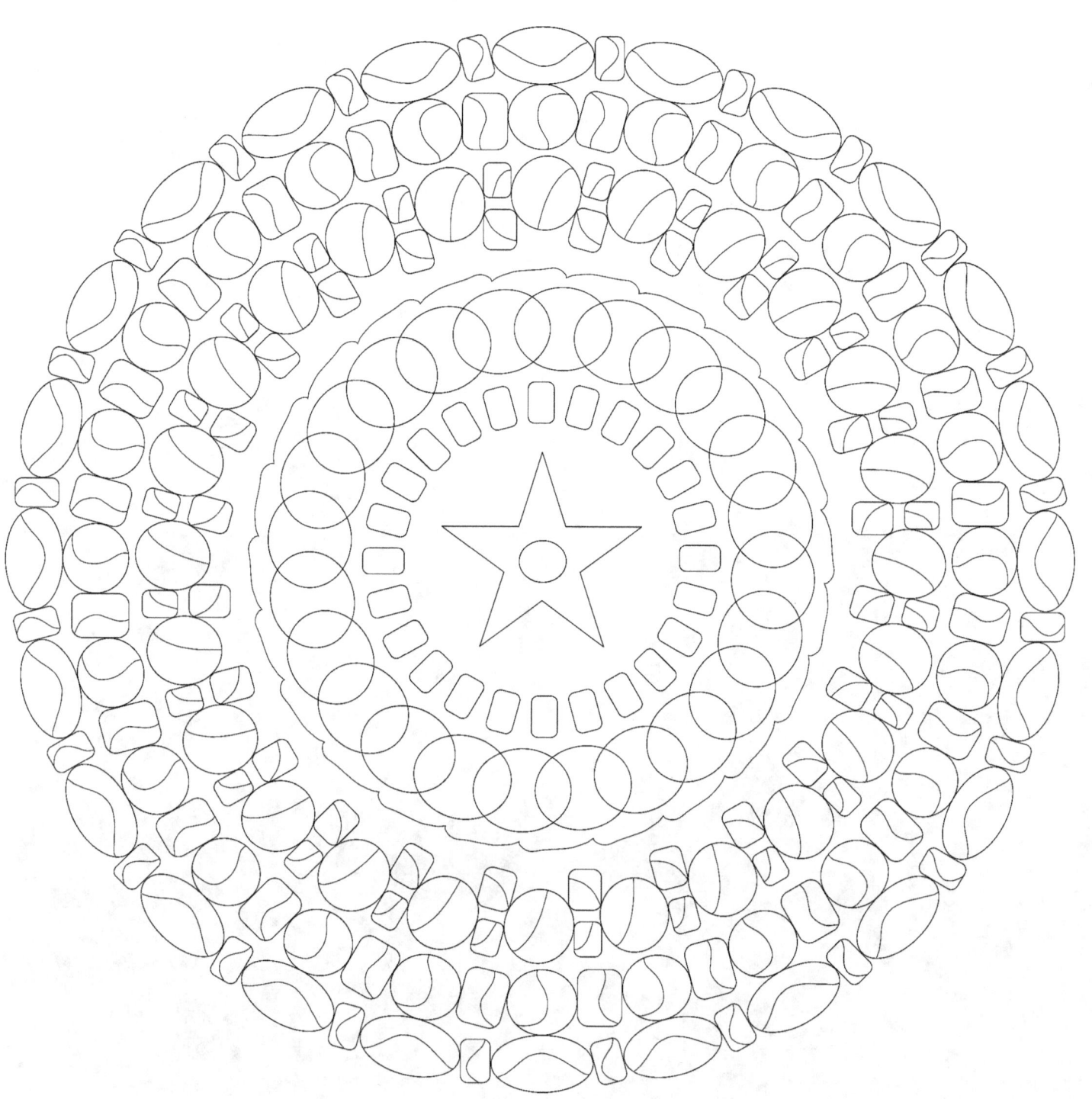

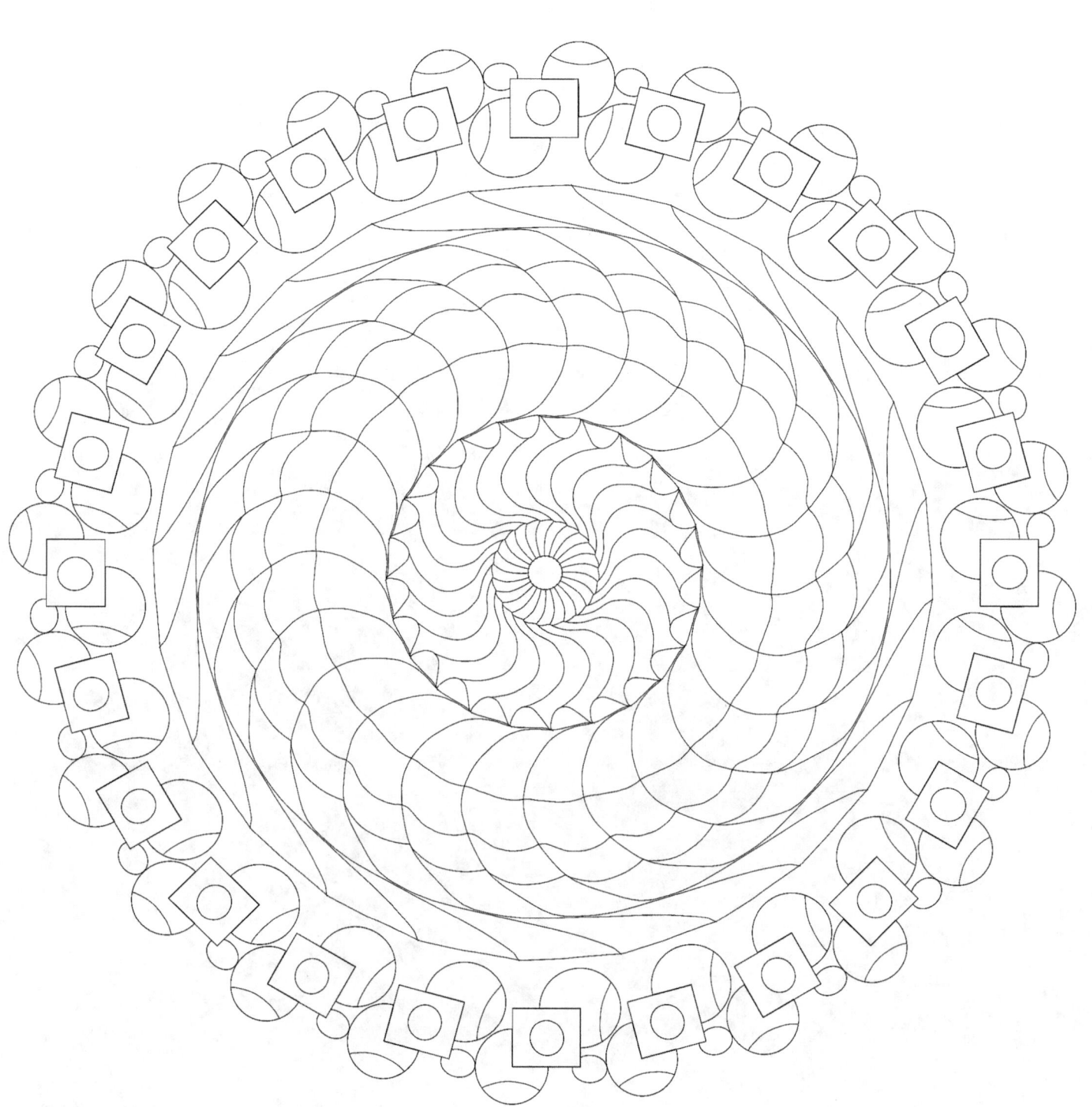

www.ingramcontent.com/pod-product-compliance
Lightning Source LLC
Chambersburg PA
CBHW081139170526
45165CB00008B/2733

* 9 7 8 1 5 4 8 6 2 9 1 3 7 *